# Equatorial Africa

**MANAGING EDITORS**
Amy Bauman
Barbara J. Behm

**CONTENT EDITORS**
Amanda Barrickman
James I. Clark
Patricia Lantier
Charles P. Milne, Jr.
Katherine C. Noonan
Christine Snyder
Gary Turbak
William M. Vogt
Denise A. Wenger
Harold L. Willis
John Wolf

**ASSISTANT EDITORS**
Ann Angel
Michelle Dambeck
Barbara Murray
Renee Prink
Andrea J. Schneider

**INDEXER**
James I. Clark

**ART/PRODUCTION**
Suzanne Beck, Art Director
Andrew Rupniewski, Production Manager
Eileen Rickey, Typesetter

Library of Congress Number: 88-18337

2  3  4  5  6  7  8  9  0    97  96  95  94  93  92


**Library of Congress Cataloging-in-Publication Data**

Pandolfi, Massimo, 1944-
   [Africa equatoriale. English]
   Equatorial Africa / Massimo Pandolfi.

   — (World nature encyclopedia)
   Translation of: Africa equatoriale
   Includes index.
   Summary: Discusses the natural and ecological niches,
boundaries, and plant and animal life of the wildlife habitats
of equatorial Africa.
   1. Ecology—Africa, Central—Juvenile literature.  2. Biotic
communities—Africa, Central—Juvenile literature.
[1. Ecology—Africa, Central.  2. Biotic communities—
Africa, Central.]  I. Title.  II. Series: Natura nel mondo.
English.
QH195.C37P3613   1988   574.5′2623′0967—dc19   88-18454
ISBN 0-8172-3325-3

WORLD NATURE ENCYCLOPEDIA

# Equatorial Africa

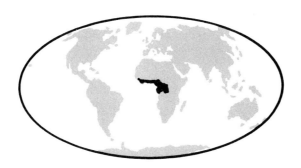

Massimo Pandolfi

RAINTREE
STECK-VAUGHN
L I B R A R Y

Austin, Texas

# CONTENTS

## INTRODUCTION

Millions of years ago, a giant forest covered all of Africa. Today, all that remains is the vast, green rain forest located near the equator. It is smaller than it once was. But this territory is still immense, fascinating, and mostly unexplored. Giant trees that tower 164 feet (50 meters) into the air grow in the equatorial forest. Their leafy tops rise up like mountain peaks. To explore this area, travelers must hack a path through the thick foliage that hides the forest's abundant wildlife.

The tropical forest is the oldest environment on earth. Its appearance has remained unchanged for more than 65 million years. Thousands of species of plants and animals whose first home was the forest survive here. They have now spread to the tropics and the temperate climates of the world. More species of plants and animals are found in the rain forest than in any other environment. Some of these species have not changed for thousands of years. Others have changed greatly in order to survive their difficult environments.

Scientists are drawn to the forest because they know that much still remains to be discovered there. Explorers continue to search for the heart of the rain forest. But trees, plants, and insects are great obstacles. In a way, scientists and researchers are much like the explorers. They try to discover how different species grow and survive in the forest. Their path is very difficult, but their discoveries are fascinating and often very helpful to people.

Animals are difficult to study in such an environment. Predators and prey are so skilled at hiding that they are almost impossible to spot. Many of these are often active only at night and hunt by ambushing or stalking. As well, many forest animals are used to living alone. They join with others only during their brief mating periods.

Still, plant and animal life is plentiful in the equatorial forest. The forest is a rich environment, whether a person wishes to study nature or just marvel at its beauty. It holds many rewards for those who take the challenge and seek to learn more about it.

# THE EQUATORIAL FOREST OF AFRICA

The African equatorial forest belongs to one of the most ancient forest systems on earth. It is known as the equatorial (or intertropical) rain forest. It extends over the "hot" zone that spans the equator between the Tropic of Cancer and the Tropic of Capricorn. This is the rainiest area on earth. Equatorial forests are found in South and Central America, Africa, Madagascar, Southeast Asia, the Indonesian islands, New Guinea, and the tropical islands of Oceania.

## Geographic Distribution

Plants of the equatorial forest are survivors from ancient times. Among these plants are families and genuses of flowers that grow in tropical areas all over the world. This planet-wide distribution of plant species is proof that the equatorial forest already existed 65 million years ago. At that time, earth's continents formed a single land mass. It was Pangaea. Later, this land mass broke apart in huge sections. It formed the bodies of land now called continents.

Cycads and Gnetinae are among the ancient plants that grow today in the humid equatorial forests. Certain tree ferns also found there are believed to be the oldest forest plant. Today, most of these plants are being replaced by flowering plants. These evolved during the Cretaceous Period, between 65 and 135 million years ago.

In Africa, the rain forest covers two regions in the west-central part of the continent. It faces the Atlantic Ocean along the Gulf of Guinea. The two regions are separated by a grassy plain, called a "savannah," and are quite different in size.

The larger region is the Gabon-Congo forest. It covers the central Congo River basin and lower Niger. It also spreads into Nigeria, Cameroon, Gabon, and Zaire. This forest extends east to the edges of the lofty central African heights (including Mount Ruwenzori), which run along a north-south line. Behind the central African heights are the great African lakes. To the south, the equatorial forest only spans the equator for a few degrees. It does not extend far over the equator into the low Congo basin. In contrast, the equatorial rain forest of America is most developed south of the equator.

The smaller region is the West African humid equatorial forest system. It covers southern Ghana, the Ivory Coast, part of upper Guinea, Liberia, and part of Sierra Leone. It is separated from the Gabon-Congo forest by the lower

*Preceding pages:* The Nigerian tropical rain forest is like a huge green ocean. Tall oil palm trees pierce the canopy, their leaves spreading out like feathers. The entire Niger Delta was a plush rain forest like this one before people began clearing it for farming and logging. Those industries caused the forest to dwindle.

*Opposite:* A waterway winds through the Mount Hoyo forest in northern Zaire. Winding rivers are often the only breaks in the dense equatorial forest. By traveling on these rivers, visitors can enter the interior of the forest. Foot paths are soon overgrown by the tangle of plant life.

regions of Benin and Togo. These regions contain savannahs and strips of ruined, open tropical forest.

The coast of Benin and Togo has no rain forests. This is probably because this stretch of Atlantic coast lies parallel to the direction of the winds which carry rain from the ocean.

## Climatic Conditions

The rain forest thrives where the climate is the same throughout the year, hot and humid. In some areas, the only climate change in the year is a single, brief season of less rainy or almost dry weather.

In the rain forest, temperatures are fairly steady throughout the year. The mean annual temperature, or the mid point between the annual temperature extremes, is between 79° and 81° Fahrenheit (26° to 27° Celsius). Those temperatures are also the average monthly temperatures.

Moisture that falls as rain, hail, and snow is called precipitation. Precipitation in the form of rain is abundant in the equatorial regions. More than 59 to 67 inches (1,500 to 1,700 millimeters) of precipitation fall annually. Rainfall often reaches up to 79 inches (2,000 mm) per year. In some

A lowland marsh in Zaire is pictured. It is not unusual for large sections of lowlands in the rain forest to be flooded. Only a few species of trees can survive with their roots under water. Many land animals adapt to these semi-marsh areas and learn to live in the water.

regions, annual rainfall measures as much as 156 to 273 inches (4,000 to 7,000 mm). Although the amount of precipitation may change from year to year, it is always abundant. This steady, high level of rainfall is the reason that the forest exists here.

In true rain forests, rainfall is as regular each day as it is throughout the year. This pattern is only interrupted during a brief dry period. The dry period lasts no longer than two months. It usually occurs during December and January.

True rain forests always appear green. New leaves grow on the trees throughout the year. A different kind of forest exists in humid equatorial regions where the drier season lasts up to three months. In these regions, some trees are deciduous. Deciduous trees are those that drop their leaves and fruit at the end of the dry season. Because of this characteristic, the forests are called "semideciduous." They are also said to be "tropophytic." This means they have adapted to the area's dry periods. These forests feature special genuses and species of plants.

An endless variety of plant life thrives in the heat and humidity of rain forests. In the past, travelers and novelists

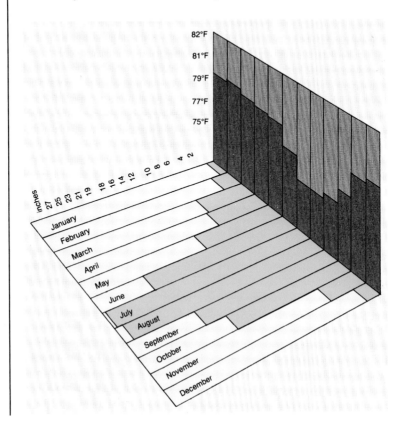

In the graph, temperature changes are shown in red, and rainfall is shown in blue. The climate in the interior of the equatorial forest is very steady. The pattern of rainfall is not so regular. Dry seasons may occur. In the rain forests, the dry season lasts two months. In the seasonal tropical forest, the dry season lasts for three months.

11

*Below:* An elephant stands at the edge of a regrown forest in Zambia. Typical savannah animals roam in this environment: hippopotamuses, elephants, and gazelles. Trees and plants that thrive in the rain forest do not grow again once the rain forest is destroyed. A different plant system, known as secondary forest, takes over. Fewer species of plants and fewer animals find homes there. Many fascinating species die off.

*Opposite:* A diagram shows the five main levels of the rain forest. The top level consists of tall trees, some 200 feet (60 m) high. They soar above the second level which is a thick cover of foliage called the canopy. The middle layer contains trees whose tapering leaves reach out in search of light. Shrubs, young plants, and sparse grasses make up the lower two levels.

called the tropical forest a "green hell." This is because thick shrubs, ferns, and cable-like tangles of vines called "lianas" grow everywhere. Lianas make walking almost impossible.

"Green hell" is not a fitting description for the original, natural equatorial forest. In the original forest, underbrush was sparse because only a small amount of light reached through the forest's thick treetops. That name better fits the secondary forest which grew after people destroyed the virgin forest. A secondary forest has thin trees with fewer leaves. These trees allow sunlight to reach the forest floor. As a result, the underbrush grows wildly and covers the forest floor.

The equatorial forest is often described as indestructible. In reality, the forest is a very fragile plant environment. It is an environment with its future threatened by the work of humans. Once the primary forest is destroyed, it becomes a scrub or secondary forest. It grows again to its original form

tallest tree level

canopy

middle level

shrub level

"grassy level"

only after a very long time. It does not recover like forests in temperate zones. Temperate forests are able to grow again after normal logging or construction activities are completed.

Often, disturbed rain forests die out completely. Instead of being replaced by scrub trees, they are replaced by savannah or grasslands where trees occasionally dot the landscape. This drastic change happens when a primary forest is located in a less rainy climate or in a climate which has a dry season.

## Characteristics of the Equatorial Forest and Its Plants

The rain forest is an enormous mass of vegetation formed by various sized trees, lianas, and shrubs. Plants called "epiphytes" compete for the little available light in the forest. Epiphytes are plants that take moisture and nutrients from the air and rain. They usually grow on other plants. In the rain forest, these plants use the air space halfway up the forest structure. They fill in spaces between the tree trunks. From the open savannah near the forest's edge, the plants look like a solid wall of green.

The rain forest is unlike other types of forests because it features several different levels of plant growth. The uppermost level is where the tallest trees grow. They stand 197 to 230 feet (60 to 70 m) above the forest floor. Next is the canopy, a thick cover that spreads like a green umbrella

13

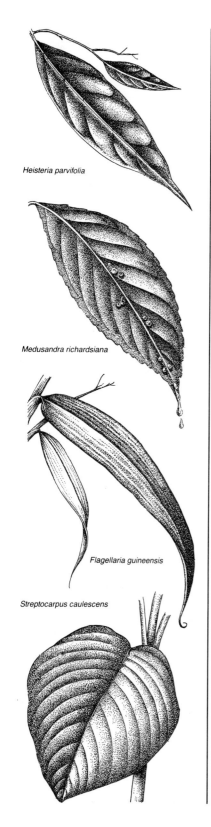

*Heisteria parvifolia*

*Medusandra richardsiana*

*Flagellaria guineensis*

*Streptocarpus caulescens*

over the forest. The canopy's foliage grows to heights of 115 feet (35 m). Below the treetops and upper canopy, a third level of vegetation grows. At this level, trees are between 33 and 98 feet (10 to 30 m) tall. Each tree's foliage is long and tapered so that excess water pours off easily. This type of foliage makes use of the little space available at that level. A fourth level of trees does not grow higher than 26 feet (8 m). It receives only a limited amount of light and grows slowly. However, when a dead tree falls, the canopy above is opened. The light causes these lower level trees to grow quickly.

The lowest layer is made up of shrubs and young trees of various species. Because of the deep shade, these plants grow as scattered underbrush, like other nonwoody plants. In this last layer, mosses grow. They do not grow as an actual layer but are scattered sparsely on tree trunks and rocks.

Even the structure of rain forest trees is different from those in temperate latitudes. Differences are particularly noticeable in the trunks, branches, and leaves. Even the flowers have unusual characteristics.

Trees that make up the canopy level have straight, thin trunks. Branches grow only at the upper parts. The bark is usually smooth and rarely cracked. It is often only an inch or two thick. Typically, these trees have flying buttresses which grow out from the base of their trunks. Flying buttresses support trees like props. On some tree trunks, trellises of aerial roots grow around the base.

These growths at the trunks are adaptations that help balance and support tall trees. They also help trees release oxygen through respiration when the soil is soaked with water. In temperate zone forests, people often identify trees by their leaves, fruit, or flowers. In tropical forests, these parts are too high to reach and examine easily. So trees are identified by the shape of the trunk. The shape is different for each genus and species.

In the field, leaves, fruit, and flowers are not good clues to the identity of a species. Different tree species in these forests have similar leaves and foliage forms. In general, they have single, broad, oblong leaves that taper to a sharp point at the tip. Water quickly runs off these leaves and thus prevents rotting. This shape allows stomata, or openings, on the leaf to expel water and continue the process of respiration. Through respiration, plants exchange gases with the atmosphere.

*Right:* The royal poinciana belongs to the Senna family. It is named for the brilliant bright red of its flowers. This beautiful equatorial species is often used as an ornamental tree in European gardens and on tree-lined avenues.

*Opposite:* To cope with heavy rains, the leaves of rain forest trees have tips like pitcher spouts. A drip tip keeps water from collecting on the leaf's surface. In such a rainy climate, leaves might rot if water did not run off. Various types of leaves in the rain forest look alike because of this feature.

Broad leaves with pointed tips are common on trees and shrubs of the forest. But they also are found on nonwoody plants of the underbrush like grasses and sedges. In temperate climates, these plants have very narrow, elongated leaves.

In the trees of the rain forest, it is common to see flowers growing directly out of a trunk or large branch. This unusual type of flowering is called "cauliflory." Farther north, this characteristic is rare but does exist. For example, in southern European temperate zones, the Judas tree flowers this

15

way. This tree and the carob, which also grows in Europe, are members of the Senna family. The Senna family is widespread in intertropical forests.

Lianas and epiphytes are plants which make the rain forest complex and interesting. Lianas are the thick cable-like vines that grow in the rain forest. They are sometimes found in deciduous or evergreen forests in temperate zones. Most commonly, they grow in equatorial rain forests. There they grow to huge sizes. Some of the largest lianas can coil around trunks at the canopy level. They grow up to 650 feet (200 m) long and 8 inches (20 centimeters) in diameter.

Lianas of the rain forest are so abundant that they make up almost nine-tenths of all the species of woody vines in the world. Where the forest is thinned out or changed in some way by people, lianas are very abundant. But in primary forests, they tend to remain dormant and do not grow in the dark and humid lower levels. When the forest is opened up for some reason, lianas are exposed to the sun's rays. They grow and climb rapidly, twining and coiling among the tree branches. Lianas are always abundant near the edge of the forest since sunlight is plentiful there.

Riverbanks also provide places that favor growth. These lianas hang in large nets that fall from the high foliage of trees. Sometimes a branch hangs out over the narrow part of a river. Then, lianas grow out and touch an overhanging branch from the opposite riverbank. Eventually, liana vines form a hanging "tunnel" between the two riverbanks.

The roots of epiphytes, or air plants, never touch the ground. Instead, these shrub-like plants attach themselves to trunks and branches of other plants. They grow wherever they find the light and moisture they need. One air plant, the heliophyte, is found at the upper canopy level of the rain forest. It has hard, fleshy leaves which allow it to survive the dryness and the heat at this height.

Plants that are parasites feed off of other plants. Epiphytes are not parasites because they use tree branches only for support. Their nourishment comes from the minerals contained in tiny soil particles. These particles become trapped near them on the tree branches. This small amount of soil is enriched by the plant's own dead leaves.

Obtaining water is difficult for an epiphyte. The small amount of soil near each plant holds only a tiny amount of moisture. For an epiphyte, the keys to survival are its own roots, a steady rainfall, and high humidity. To obtain water,

*Opposite:* The edge of the forest is seen in the Ituri region in Zaire. Twisting vine-like lianas take advantage of the light in these places and grow abundantly. They coil in intricate nets around the trunks and branches. In the shady depths of the forest where the canopy is thick, they do not grow. They remain dormant.

The pygmies of Zaire make their homes in the equatorial forest. They are experts at identifying numerous species of trees that share their natural habitat. The pygmies do not use leaves and fruit to recognize a species. Those parts of a tree are out of reach in the tall forest. Instead, they look at, smell, and sometimes taste the trunk and roots before coming to a decision. Scientists have learned much about the forest from these local experts.

the epiphyte catches rain in its long, thick tangle of exposed roots. These roots also absorb humidity from the air itself. In some species, the epiphyte's leaves are cupped and can hold a small supply of water.

Epiphytes common to more humid rain forests are seldom found in forests where seasons change drastically. These plants cannot survive drier seasons.

Plants such as lichens, mosses, and algae grow at all levels of the rain forest. They are found on trees as well as on rocks. These endless types of fungi with strange shapes and colors are found everywhere. They grow in the soil, on fallen leaves, and on tree trunks and branches. They are extremely important to the life of the forest. They join with decaying leaves and other matter from trees and plants. Together they

form minerals necessary for young plants to begin sprouting. These minerals also keep giant trees growing.

The rain forest is green throughout the year. The cycle of flowering, reproduction, fruiting, and budding is not interrupted by changing seasons. Without constant heat, high humidity, and the presence of broadleaf trees, the cycle would stop.

Usually, leaves remain on a tree for a little over a year. Then the tree sheds them. In a short time, new growth covers the tree. Each tree drops its leaves and buds again on its own schedule. So there is never a time when all trees are bare. When a tree is cut down in a temperate forest, the stump shows many growth rings. A person can figure the tree's age by counting the growth rings in the stump. Each ring shows how much the tree grew during a single growing season. In the rain forest, the climate is even throughout the year. Because of this, there are no growth rings in tree wood. This is especially true of trees that grow at the lower levels where the climate never changes.

## The Complex Forest Trees

Botanists who study temperate forests are amazed by the many tree species in a tropical forest. For example, a forest area covering 165 feet x 165 feet (50 m x 50 m) in a temperate zone may feature ten different tree species. The same sized forest in a tropical zone may feature thirty to forty different species. In an area large enough to find fifteen species of trees in a temperate forest, botanists might find as many as 100 to 150 different species in a tropical forest.

Is it possible to identify the many trees in the tropical forest? Some forest dwellers, like the pygmies of the Ituri region, are masters of identification. For them, the equatorial forest northeast of Zaire has always been home. They can recognize almost every one of the hundreds of different species of trees in the forest. Unlike a typical botanist, pygmies do not examine leaves, flowers, and fruit to identify a species. They cannot look at these parts closely because the parts are hidden in the thick forest canopy. They are also too high to reach. Even a forest dweller has difficulty climbing to the closest branches. Some of these may be 65 to 100 feet (20 to 30 m) off the ground.

To identify the various species, pygmies use all of their senses. First, they closely examine the bark. They also may cut off a piece to look at the wood underneath the bark. They notice the color, smell, and even the taste by chewing

This small tree, the *Cola digitata,* grows in the lower levels of the forest. There its reddish purple fruit and blue seeds are visible. Its relative is the cacao tree. Both are members of the Sterculiad family. Like other members of that group, the *cola digitatas* seeds contain caffeine, theine, and theobromine, which are stimulants. Local people use them like coffee beans.

*Opposite:* One of the most common plant species of the African equatorial forests is the *Lophira alata.* At the top of the drawing, the whole tree is shown. In the middle, the drawing shows a flowering branch. This tree is easier to see because it is one of the tallest trees that rises above the canopy. At the bottom is the staghorn fern which grows on long branches in the forest's middle layer. The long leaves of this air plant, or epiphyte, may be 24 inches (60 cm) long.

Lophira alata

staghorn fern

a piece for its flavor. Finally, they come to a decision. When their opinions are checked scientifically, pygmies usually are found to be correct. Botanists studying the rain forest often talk to the natives. They make use of the natives' extraordinary firsthand knowledge of trees.

Trees are like friendly neighbors to local people. For them, learning about the trees and naming them is natural. In fact, the people not only have names for the trees, but they also call the flowering, fruiting, and budding cycles of different species by different names.

## Floral Composition

Tropical forests generally do not support the same plant life everywhere. This is true of Africa's humid equatorial forest, too. Some species are confined to certain areas within the vast rain forest. It seems as though the same climate would be everywhere in the rain forest. But differences exist. It is possible for a particular section to have a slightly different soil or humidity level than the rest of the rain forest. Those different conditions may provide the perfect environment for a particular plant. Eventually, specific species take over, or dominate, certain sections of the forest.

One environment where specific species dominate is the forest system of the Ivory Coast. Botanists call it the *Uapaca* forest group. Within the Uapaca forest region, there are also some smaller tree groups. Two of them are the *Mapania* and *Turreanthus* trees. *Mapania* trees grow best on low, humid plains and valleys where the soil is mainly clay. This soil has developed over time from the decomposition of crystalline rock. In these areas, large trees of the sedge family and the species *Heritiera hutilis*, or *niangon* tree, are widespread. The niangon's wood is considered to be very valuable. It is commonly used in the Ivory Coast.

Sandy soil that drains better than clay produces a different species. *Turreanthus* trees grow on this type of soil. They do well in a less humid environment that *Mapania* trees.

Large, woody lianas and creeping palms are found everywhere in the West African rain forest. Arums are also common. This plant is semiepiphytic, which means its roots are partly exposed to the air.

As in other parts of the forest, different air plants grow under various soil and moisture conditions. Some of the higher epiphytes are called "xerophytes." They are plants which can stand drier climates. Xerophytes that grow in

Dawn comes to the Wassa region of Zaire's equatorial forest. Here, as elsewhere, many living things interact with each other and their surroundings. Together these interactions make up an ecosystem. In the rain forest, there are more species for each section of land than in any other ecosystem on earth. Because plants and animals are so numerous, competition among them is very intense. No one species can dominate over another as species do in the woods of temperate forests. Compared to woods where a species such as pine trees dominates, the equatorial forest with its mix of plants and trees may seem disorderly.

this region are orchids and certain fig shrubs.

Other plants, called "hygrophytes," are found where moisture is plentiful. Ferns are the most common of these rain-loving plants. Lower epiphytes fall into this category. These species grow in valleys and mountain forests where ferns of the genus *Trichomanes*, mosses, and liverworts grow in abundance. Two types of ferns, the staghorn fern (*Platycerium*) and *Drynaria*, grow in dryer areas of the rain forest.

The rain forest is never dry, but there are parts that are less rainy. One of these drier areas lies north of West Africa's constantly green rain forests. Here many seasonal tropical, or semideciduous, forests grow. Numerous species found in these drier forests also are found in *Uapaca* forests. But several species, such as various species of *Celtis*, grow only in this seasonal tropical forest.

In the Congo River basin region, the true rain forest makes up the core of the forest system. Surrounding it are huge areas where seasonal forests alternate with tunnel forests. Tunnel forests grow along riverbanks. They are called "tunnel forests" because they follow the river. Strips of savannah grow between the forests.

In some forests, one species is dominant. The dominant plant grows in great numbers. This affects the type and number of other plants that grow in the area. The *Brachystegia laurenti* is such a tree. The largest trees of this species reach enormous dimensions. They grow to be 150 to 165 feet (45 to 50 m) tall. Trunks grow as high as 66 feet (20 m) before branching. In this forest, 60 percent of the canopy level is made up of *Brachystegia laurenti*. Two hundred other species make up the remaining 40 percent.

The forests of Cameroon in the upper Cross River basin support numerous trees of the Senna family (*Caesalpiniaceae*). They include *Afzelia bella, Anthomotha fragrans,* and *Brachystegia cynometroides*. Different forest groupings grow along the coasts. The main species are the *Sacoglottis gabonensis, Lophira alata,* and *Cynometra hankei*.

In Gabon, rain forests produce numerous Gaboon mahogany trees that are known locally as "okoume." Because the mahogany wood is highly valued, Gabon has profited by its sale. Usually when people cut down virgin forest, secondary forest replaces it. Valuable trees do not grow back for a very long time, and the forest is not as dense. In the case of the Gaboon mahogany, the opposite is true. More of these valued mahogany trees can grow in a secondary forest. Because the regrown forest is not dense, it allows more light. The mahogany trees need a great deal of light. Thus, they do very well in a secondary forest.

Like the West African forest system, the Congolese forest is surrounded by a seasonal tropical forest. Beyond that forest zone are the grasslands. Also found in these outer forests are various types of flowers.

## The Soil of the Rain Forest

The soil of the equatorial forest is built up of animal and plant matter, minerals, and the air. It can be very deep, over 33 feet (10 m).

Because of the constant humidity and high temperatures, the rocky subsoil of the equatorial forest decomposes quickly. It releases large amounts of iron oxide. This mineral gives the African soil a typical brick red color that visitors find striking. In fact, the name of this type of soil,

An old laterite pit in Cameroon shows how the work of human beings changes the forest. The rain forest soil is normally very fertile and deep. It is also extremely delicate. Soon after its green cover is stripped away, it quickly deteriorates. Heavy rains wash nutrients out of exposed soil. The strong sun completes the destruction by drying out the surface. Then evaporation causes salts and oxides to rise to the soil surface from lower layers. Finally, the once-moist soil becomes a hard crust.

*laterite,* comes from the Latin word for brick.

The forest floor in temperate forests is covered with a thick layer of dry leaves, dead branches, and other plant matter. This protective layer does not exist in the rain forest where leaves and other plant matter decompose so quickly.

Though it may seem amazing, the rain forest soil is actually very poor in nutrients. If a plant's roots do not absorb minerals immediately, they are quickly washed away by heavy rains. The soil has no clay or thick layer of decayed plant matter, called humus, to trap minerals.

With such poor soil, why are plants so plentiful in the rain forest? Compared to temperate forests, an entirely different system is present. Tropical plant roots do not burrow deep in the soil for their food. Instead, they get necessary phosphorus, potassium, calcium, magnesium, and other nutrients from the decay of dead animals and plants. When the delicate balance of life is disturbed, these fragile plants

When rain forests are cleared for farming, the same vegetation does not grow again. This drawing shows the plant cycle after rain forest land is used and abandoned by farmers. First, the farmer clears the land by burning off the existing trees and plants. The cultivated land quickly loses its nutrients. The farmer then leaves it to seek new areas to cultivate. A secondary forest, where oil palm trees grow well, takes the place of the original rain forest. The cycle starts again when the farmer cuts down trees, clears the land, and plants crops, Only the oil palms are left standing because their products can be sold. Soon the soil does not produce crops and the farmer abandons it. The next forest that grows on the land has even fewer species than the last. After the next farming cycle, only grasslands cover the land.

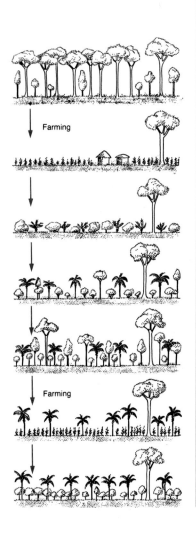

are destroyed. Once the roots are cut, the forest dies and will not grow again. The soil is quickly stripped of nutrients and cannot support plant life.

## Use of the Rain Forest and Its Soil

All over the world, people are cutting down trees in rain forests. This process is called "deforestation." In equatorial Africa, rain forests are being destroyed so that the land can be used for farming. Yet, because the soil is so poor, crops can only be grown for two or three years. When the soil is no longer productive, farmers simply clear more forest land. Even forests planted after the destruction of the original rain forest are being wiped out. In the end, neither trees nor crops can grow on the land. Abandoned areas may become desert.

When people cut down a forest, they often leave some trees standing. Some trees are saved because they provide shade. Others are saved for their fruit. Some trees have a special place in the traditions or customs of a particular tribe or village. But even trees that are chopped down are put to use. First, the logs are left to dry. Later they are burned. Their ashes are spread over farmland because they are rich in soil nutrients. But this source of plant food is quickly used. After a few years, farmers find that their crops are dwindling. The fragile topsoil is gone. Plants have absorbed most of the soil's nutrients. Soon the people realize that more farming would be unproductive. Once again, they leave the land barren.

Sometimes abandoned land is taken over by wild scrub plants. Later, farmers seek out this land. They clear it and plant crops until the land no longer yields well.

In some areas, forests do regrow on abandoned land. But only a few types of plants and animals survive compared to the large variety found in the rain forest. Regrowth occurs in areas where the climate has a regular rainfall and no dry season. Sometimes the soil has been farmed without breaks between harvests. Then only scrub vegetation or very young secondary forest will grow again.

Farming has a different effect on land where seasonal, or semideciduous, tropical forest once grew. During the three-month dry season, fires sweep across the land and destroy young trees. Laterite, or iron oxide, is drawn up to the surface when water evaporates. This causes a hard crust to form on the soil's surface. Without trees to protect it, the soil becomes very hard. Here woody forests or shrubs do not regrow. Instead, only grassy plants will grow. The land

becomes a savannah.

The rainy season lasts most of the year. Heavy rains fall on the bare, sloping ground in the deforested areas. These rains cause the soil to be so completely eroded that the land becomes desert.

Farming and logging are two uses of deforested land. These uses have completely changed vast areas of land in equatorial Africa. Green rain forests have disappeared. In their place, only scrub plants and small trees of the secondary forest grow. In many regions, these species are even taking over the true rain forest.

## An Urgent Conservation Problem

The tropical forest is a precious resource. No other system of living things on earth has a greater number of animal and plant species. Scientists estimate that there are 250,000 species of flowering plants in the world. Most of them are found in tropical regions. In South and Central America, there are at least ninety thousand species. In tropical Africa, there are thirty thousand species.

Each year thousands of acres of the world's tropical forests are destroyed. The lush plant life in these forests makes up almost half of the world's plant species. Though the numbers are large, the balance of life of the forest environment is easily upset. Once the shallow root systems are cut, the forest dies quickly. Until recently, the world's

This view shows a savannah area in Kenya after a fire. The savannah, or grassland where only a few small trees grow, replaces what was once an equatorial rain forest. After the equatorial forest is cut down several times for farming or logging, only savannahs grow back. The area eventually becomes a semidesert region.

27

Plant species that grow naturally in the forest are shown at the edge of the forest. To the left of the thin diagonal stream that cuts across the open area, shrubby plants are taking over abandoned farmland. In the area to the right of the stream, many tree trunks can be seen. These tree trunks suggest that just a few months before this picture was taken, the area was a rain forest.

28

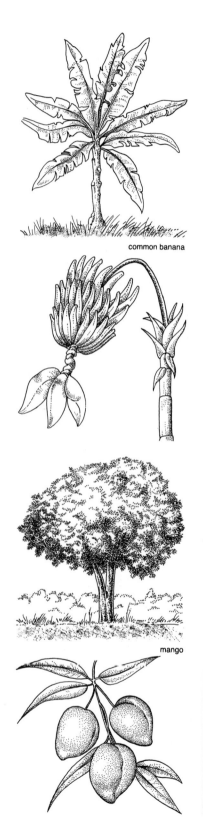

common banana

mango

tropical forests covered 4,478,760 square miles (11,600,000 square kilometers). Presently, about 44,000 sq. miles (114,000 sq. km) are being destroyed each year. That area is almost equal to the size of Greece. Scientists predict that within twenty to fifty years, the rain forest will completely disappear. These scientists are demanding that this destruction be halted before it is too late.

The predictions are already becoming fact in some areas. In Africa, one unfortunate example exists in the Ivory Coast. That country destroys 1,930 sq. miles (5,000 sq. km) of tropical forest each year. The exportation and sale of the wood is very profitable. Today, products from forests make up 12 percent of the Ivory Coast's exports. By 1990, forests of the Ivory Coast will be gone completely. The country will be without the income it now makes from the sale of tree products. It will have destroyed the forest from which they came. In the end, the barren land may create worse and more expensive problems. Similar deforestation problems exist in Brazil. Brazil has the largest forest surface of any country in the entire world. Each year, it destroys as many as 5,636 sq. miles (14,600 sq. km) of forest.

For many years, scientists have explained that the survival of the tropical forest may mean the survival of people. They conclude that the destruction of forests is the most serious ecological catastrophe that could hit the earth.

Scientists know that everyone on earth lives in the same biosphere. The biosphere is the part of the world in which life can exist. Earth's biosphere includes the atmosphere and the oceans. The tropical forest system plays an important role in the biosphere. The biosphere works like a giant factory. Its plentiful plant life produces enormous amounts of oxygen and moisture. These products cool and provide air for earth's life forms. When fragile tropical forests disappear, the plant life that traps moisture disappears. Rainwater runs to the sea without evaporating into the air. Soil washes away from constant erosion. Finally, the earth's climate becomes hotter and its lands drier.

Possibly, this destruction began with primitive people one hundred thousand years ago. African hunter gatherers once roamed over forests that grew where the vast Sahara Desert exists today. Primitive rock paintings in the Sahara picture forests that once grew there. They show leopards, hippopotamuses, elephants, and giraffes. These species only survive in more humid climates.

*Below:* Until the middle of the twentieth century, the rain forest managed to survive despite efforts to use that land for growing and logging. Until then, people who cut down the forest allowed enough time for plant cover to regrow. However, in the last forty years, the logging industry, mining, and agriculture have expanded. More rain forest land has been used for these operations. Now, the survival of the rain forest itself is threatened. Green areas on the map show the distribution of tropical forest in 1975. The red areas show where deforestation, or the destruction of the forest, is occurring. Below, the box graph tells how much of earth's land was rain forest in 1950 and in 1975. Rain forest regions are being rapidly wiped out. By the year 2000, only 7 percent of the land will be rain forest.

How could primitive people wipe out the forest? The answer is fire. Primitive hunters or shepherds used this powerful weapon on a huge scale to drive animals out of the forest for slaughter. Herders wanted to clear the forest so that grasses would grow for grazing. As thousands of years passed, the land became drier and drier until desert took over.

Many people believe that it is wrong to destroy the rain forest. For one thing, it is the natural home to many people. Natives, like the pygmies, live in harmony with the forest. They have a right to go on living there and to follow their own customs. Clearly, their way of life will not survive if they are forced to become farmers, loggers, or factory workers. The large primates are also dwellers of the equatorial forest. This group of animals, which includes gorillas, chimpanzees, and arboreal monkeys, faces extinction. Other large mammals in Africa also have difficulty surviving in the shrinking territories. Most land animals, including people, evolved from tropical creatures. So, in a biological sense, they all share the same heredity. People must protect these forest dwellers and keep them alive.

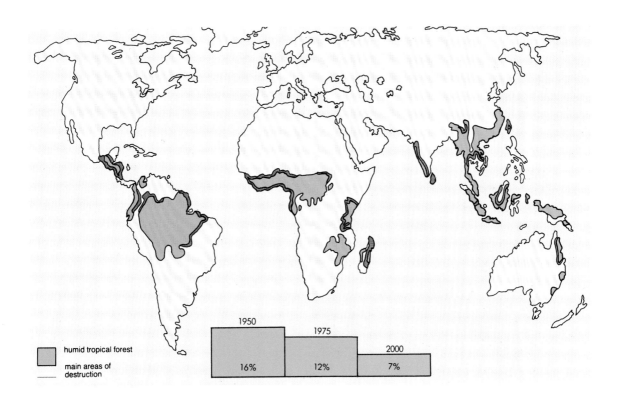

humid tropical forest

main areas of destruction

1950 — 16%

1975 — 12%

2000 — 7%

# THE RULERS OF THE CANOPY

To catch sight of gnus, gazelles, and zebras, travelers go to the wide African savannah. There, herds of these hoofed animals make their homes. But to find monkeys, one must look to the upper branches of the rain forest trees. These rain forest animals have little use for solid ground. They spend their time in the trees of the rain forest. Some may be found just a few yards above the ground. Others are found in the treetops as high as 150 feet (45 m) from the ground. Typical small monkeys are the guenons, mangabeys, and the colobus monkeys. The colobus monkeys, which have long black-and-white hair, are also called "guerezas."

Larger monkeys, like the mandrills, chimpanzees, and gorillas, travel on the ground as well as in trees. But the arboreal, or tree-dwelling monkeys, are seldom found on the ground. These monkeys are very agile. They swing and leap easily through the tangle of trunks and branches in the rain forest. The canopy is the arboreal monkey's permanent home. There, the light is brighter, the tall trees flower more often, and fruit is plentiful.

## Arboreal Monkeys

From the sky, the forest canopy seems monotonously similar. Yet within the canopy, there are many niches in which different animals survive. The relationships that an animal has with its habitat make up its "ecological niche." A niche is both a place and what an animal does within and to its place.

Different species of monkeys have evolved and survived in the canopy's many niches. For example, more than twenty species can be found in one habitat. Within those twenty species, there can be as many as one hundred subspecies.

Monkeys are separated into two groups: Old World and New World monkeys. Old World types are found in areas such as Asia, Africa, and India. New World types are found in the Americas. The two groups have different characteristics that help them live in high treetops. For example, the Cercopithecidae (a subfamily of the Old World monkeys) have slender, elongated bodies and limbs. Their hands and long-toed feet are prehensile. This means that they are adapted for grasping. Any limb or tail that can grasp branches, vines, or anything else is called prehensile. The tails of Old World monkeys are not prehensile. But they do use their long tails for balance as they move through the branches.

*Opposite:* Two magnificent black-and-white colobus monkeys are shown in their natural habitat. Tree monkeys are typical mammals of the forest and are especially well adapted to upper trees. These small, agile animals have prehensile hands and feet for grasping branches and food. They use their long tails for balance when leaping from tree to tree. These monkeys have thrived so well in the rain forest that a number of species and subspecies can now be found there.

An animal's muzzle includes its nose, mouth, and jaw area. As shown here, the mandrills muzzle is brightly colored. Tree monkeys use color to recognize members of their own and other species. Color is also a sign of power within the group. Only adult monkeys have colored muzzles. The most powerful male has the brightest colors.

All arboreal monkeys have frontal vision. Their vision is also stereoscopic, or three-dimensional. Because of this adaptation, they can calculate depth very well. This skill is necessary as they leap quickly from branch to branch high above the ground.

Monkeys do not have a keen sense of smell or long snouts like many savannah animals. Unlike ground dwellers, monkeys do not have to detect the scent of an enemy approaching. Nor do the monkeys have to track their prey by following a scent. As a result, monkeys have lost some of their sense of smell. So, as they evolved, their snouts grew shorter. Today, arboreal monkeys depend on their sense of sight to find food. Their keen vision helps them quickly spot color changes in the dense foliage. This helps them find ripe fruit which is important to their diets.

Rain forest monkeys have bright blue, white, and red faces. Their faces look like they have been painted by an imaginative artist. But these bright colors are not just an

A female blue monkey carries her infant. Her method frees her limbs and tail for running and searching. Holding on to the mother's stomach, the baby stays in place.

exotic feature of the tropics. The color appears on the monkeys for a particular purpose. Without these colors, they might have difficulty recognizing members of their own species. Colorful species include the De Brazza's monkeys which have large, red frontal patches. The white-nosed guenons have white and blue faces. The mustached guenon is another colorful monkey. It has a blue nose, blue-rimmed eyes, and a black-rimmed mouth. This unusual monkey also has a white horizontal stripe across its face, and yellow tufts at its cheeks.

Both the faces and hindquarters of mandrills are colored in bright reds and blues. Colors play an important social role within this monkey group. Among adult males, these colors become more brilliant when they are battling for power in the group. Dominant males have the brightest colors. Other members of the group recognize the leader's power by his strong colors. Sometimes, rivals are so intimidated by the leader's impressive colors that they do not fight at all.

## The Diana Monkey: An In-Depth Study

The complex environment of the tropical forest is difficult to study. This is true for several reasons. The thick tangle of vegetation makes it impossible to travel within the forest. Obtaining transportation and supplies is difficult in

The drawing shows a few of the most common species of tree monkeys in the African equatorial forest. *Top, from left to right:* the Diana monkey, the gray-cheeked mangabey, and the black-and-white colobus monkey. *Bottom, left to right:* De Brazza's monkey, the greater white-nosed guenon, and the red colobus. In studies conducted in the Kibale Forest of Uganda, zoologists learned that groups of monkeys cooperate with one another in their search for food. Conflict and direct competition are rare between them.

many areas of Africa. So the life habits of monkeys that live deep in the forest remain a mystery.

However, two species have been studied in depth. These two are the Congo white-nosed guenon and the Diana monkey. The Diana monkey also is called the "diademed guenon." Much has been learned about these species. From this knowledge, scientists draw conclusions about how other tree monkeys live.

The Diana monkey is called the diademed guenon because white hairs grow from its forehead. The hairs, which grow in a cluster, resemble a crown, or diadem. This explains the monkey's nickname. An average-sized Diana monkey is 24 inches (60 cm) long with a 30-inch (75 cm) tail. It has a reddish brown back with a light-colored belly. This guenon is widespread through most of tropical Africa.

Many subspecies exist in the rain forest. Adult male Diana monkeys have long white vibrissae. Vibrissae are sensitive hairs located around the mouth of an animal. They are useful for "feeling" surrounding branches and trees as the monkey swings through the forest. On some parts of its body, the monkey has no hair. On the very young, bare parts of the face, hands, and feet are pink. When the monkeys are fully grown, these parts become black.

The Diana monkey shares its habitat with many other species of monkeys. The tropical forest has a wealth of ecological niches. Within these niches, different species find places and ways to survive. Diana monkeys and other monkeys find their niches on different levels of the forest. There they make best use of available resources. Like other monkeys, this guenon does not use its habitat by traveling

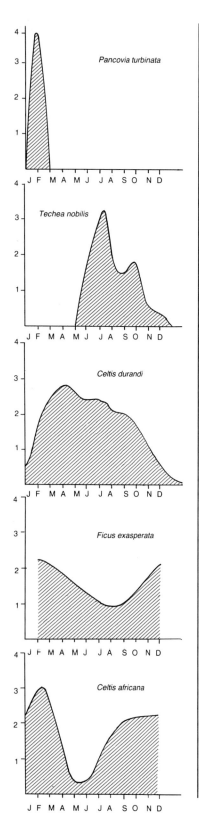

*Pancovia turbinata*

*Techea nobilis*

*Celtis durandi*

*Ficus exasperata*

*Celtis africana*

horizontally. It does not travel at the same height from tree to tree. Instead it uses levels of the forest as if they were stories in an apartment building. The guenon's habitat includes different heights of the forest. Within its habitat, many similar species may also dwell.

Tree monkeys are specialized in their eating habits. They eat at several forest levels. They also travel to other places where they compete with other species for food. Because they are specialized, two different species may coexist in the same level and area. They do this by choosing different foods for their basic nutrition. One may be a leaf-eater. Another may be a fruit-eater. The way the food source is distributed determines how arboreal monkeys use space within a particular niche. Food supply also affects the social organization of a monkey group.

Tropical vegetation does not grow only during certain seasons as in temperate zone forests. There is no particular season when all the plants sprout new leaves. Nor is there a special season for flowering and fruiting.

In studying the Kibale Forest, researchers learned that certain types of trees were very important food sources for monkeys. They calculated how many leaves, flowers, and fruit the trees produced during specific times of the year. They found that fruit production varied enormously. Some plants produced fruit all year. Others produced fruit only once every few years. It is known that trees of this species do not grow randomly here and there, but in small groups. Therefore, groups of monkeys must be constantly on the move within their territory. They must search for special trees that produce foods they need.

## Social Structure

Diana monkeys live together in social groups. A group may include between thirteen and twenty-seven animals. Rare ones who live alone are usually adult males who have no territory of their own. They constantly move from area to area, stopping only for two or three weeks. Eventually, they may find a group that they can join. But it is not easy for an adult male outsider to enter a new group.

To join a new group of monkeys, the single male must battle the leader. If the challenger wins, he is the new leader of that group. A typical tree monkey's social group includes one dominant male and a number of females, juveniles, and infants. One group of twenty-seven guenons includes one adult male, eleven adolescents and juveniles, twelve fe-

*Above:* An adult and a young guenon are shown resting in the trees. Guenons spend almost all of their time in trees. To make them more comfortable as they sit or sleep on rough bark, their hindquarters have patches of thick, leathery skin that are known as ischial callouses.

*Opposite:* Diademed guenons depend on certain plants and fruit to survive. In the diagram, the yearly growth cycles of some of the fruit is shown. A comparison of cycles shows that different species produce fruit at different times throughout the year. Each month, fruit is available from one or more species. For example, the *Pancovia turbinata* fruit is available from January to March. The *Techea nobilis* fruit is available from May to December. Monkeys travel within their territory to eat from trees that have a new supply of fruit.

males, and three infants. Females and young are clearly the majority.

The job of defending the group falls to the powerful adult male. He is so aggressive that he even treats the young males roughly, almost as enemies. When they mature, the young males leave the group. They will then form their own groups or roam alone in the forest. To an observer, the leader's behavior may seem cruel. Yet, his instinct to drive away young males is based on an important biological fact. To stay strong, species must mix their genes by mating with members outside their family groups. With a mixture of genes, individual members of a species survive better. If the young male stayed in his family group, he might mate with his own relatives. His offspring would be weak. They, in turn, would produce weaker monkeys. Eventually, the group would die out. So, by leaving the family, the young males find mates from outside the group. This keeps the species strong.

Different groups of monkeys claim different territories as their own. Each group protects its territory. Occasionally,

By observing how the blue monkeys search for food, scientists learn how tree monkey species cooperate. At times, guenons group with red colobus monkeys *(shown above)* which only eat insects. In this way, guenons benefit from the red colobus' ability to catch invertebrates. At other times, guenons join with the Congo white-nosed guenon *(shown opposite, in the drawing). This species is a strict vegetarian. It knows exactly when trees in its small area bud and bear fruit. The blue monkeys follow the white-nosed guenons, using them as a shortcut to the food supply.*

a group of monkeys crosses into another group's territory. When this happens, the two groups face each other and threaten each other with high-pitched screams. The owners of the territory pursue the intruders and drive them off. Most of the time, the battle is nothing more than a very loud shouting match and a few chases among the tree branches. No one is injured. When the intruders leave, the owners resume normal activities.

## Feeding Strategies

Each member of the group helps search for food. When one finds some appetizing fruit, for example, it calls the others. Together they scramble into those trees to feed. Usually, Diana monkeys do not wander far from their group. As they travel, they all stay within an area that measures between 240 and 1,200 sq. yards (200 to 1,000 sq. m). These very social animals even travel with other monkey species.

For example, Diana monkeys often join groups of Congo white-nosed guenons or red colobus monkeys. On occasion, they even travel with gray-cheeked mangabeys, black-and-white colobus monkeys, or De Brazza's monkeys.

Guenons are not the only animals that associate with different species. This behavior is typical of small perching birds like Eurasian goldfinches, greenfinches, linnets, serins, and others. They travel together in groups and feed together on meadows. Large hoofed animals of the savannah also form groups of mixed species. It is not unusual to see gnus, zebras, and gazelles feeding together on the plains.

This tendency is known as grouping behavior. It is common among animals that stay together throughout their lives, like herds of hoofed animals. But it is also found among those that only band together for a short time. Birds, for example, band together when they migrate. Normally, these species live in separate ecological niches. Why do they join together at certain times? Food is one reason. With more animals searching, a particular food is easier to find. Often, animals must search over a large area to find the special leaves or fruit they need. With a larger group, more territory can be covered. The search may be shorter. Another advantage is that insects are stirred up when large groups of monkeys forage through the trees. Both monkeys and birds take advantage of this food source.

Another advantage is defense. When danger is near, the signal rapidly spreads through larger groups. As the old saying goes, two eyes are better than one. When animals band together, a hundred eyes see better than ten. Because each member is watchful, the group as a whole is safer. Each member then has more time to feed.

Diana monkeys have learned that teamwork is important in searching for food. In the tropical forest, these monkeys join with red colobus monkeys to search for insects. The red colobus species is a canopy dweller. It is more skilled at finding insects than the Diana monkey. In a sense, the colobus monkeys help the others. They guide the Diana monkeys to areas where insects are more plentiful. This grouping is very beneficial to the Diana monkeys. Through it, even their young learn new things. Imitating the red colobus monkeys, the young Diana monkeys learn new ways to forage and hunt.

At other times, these guenons live on leaves and fruit instead of insects. When they search for these foods, they do not travel with red colobus monkeys. Instead, they follow

*These grasshoppers could be the prey of a tree monkey. The blue monkey is omnivorous. It eats both plants and animals. Invertebrates like these grasshoppers, spiders, and ants make up about 20 percent of the blue monkey's diet. Flowers, fruit, and leaves make up the remaining 80 percent. As with many omnivores, the diademed guenon does not feed on only one type of food, even if it is plentiful. There are advantages to this habit. First, some food is left over as a reserve supply in case of shortage. Second, the group does not become dependent on a single food which could possibly become scarce. Third, the variety provides these animals with mineral salts and vitamins they need to stay healthy.*

the Congo white-nosed guenon. This monkey inhabits a territory covering only a few square miles. Its territory is much smaller than the territory of the Diana monkey. The size of the territory affects the guenon's ability to find food. For example, the Diana monkey spends several weeks searching its large forest territory. But the white-nosed guenon combs through its territory in a few days. The white-nose has a more detailed, tree-by-tree knowledge of its area. It knows exactly when fruit begins to ripen. It also knows when trees are about to form new leaves or flower. Knowing how guenons hunt, the Diana monkey uses the white-nose as a shortcut to food. Traveling through their large territory, the Diana monkeys find the white-nosed guenons. They then simply follow the guenons to the food sources. The Diana monkeys avoid conflict by feeding at different times. The white-nosed guenons eat in the early morning. The Diana monkeys then eat later in the morning or in the afternoon.

What prey do these monkeys pursue? Even though guenons are vegetarians, insects make up a good portion of their diet. They also eat invertebrates such as grasshoppers, beetles, ants, large butterflies, and others. Invertebrates, or animals without backbones, make up 20 percent of the guenons' food. To find invertebrates, monkeys carefully examine the bark and leaves of trees. Young monkeys actually eat more invertebrates than adults do.

*Right:* The crowned eagle is the tree monkey's most feared enemy. It is called "leopard of the air" by natives. It has the broad, rounded wings and long tail that are typical of eagles that hunt in dense forests.

*Below:* Birds of prey that hunt monkeys include the monkey-eating eagle of the Philippines, the South American harpy, and the African crowned eagle. They are similar in appearance although they evolved from different species. Their bodies are especially adapted to flight in the forest. They have large claws and a strong beak. They all have a crest of plumes that rise from the crown of the head. These showy feathers move in the wind as the eagle perches in the foliage. They make these eagles hard to see clearly.

monkey-eating eagle

harpy

Tree monkeys usually leave larger animals in peace. A group of Diana monkeys was once observed for more than a year. During that time, they attacked a larger animal only once. On that occasion, a young male monkey caught and ate an African wood-owl. This young guenon never attempted to share its catch with any other member of the group. Nor did any of his companions seem to want it. Not all species of monkeys behave this way. Sometimes a chimpanzee catches a small vertebrate, such as a baby colobus monkey, guenon, or squirrel. The chimpanzee will divide its catch among the other members of the group.

In the evening, Diana monkeys return to one of their usual resting places. They do not build nests like larger monkeys such as chimpanzees and gorillas. Instead, they spend the night in very high trees. They each take a different spot, never very far from one another. Strangely, they never choose fruit trees. Perhaps Diana monkeys want to avoid the

disturbance in the fruit trees that fruit-eating bats, viverrids, and pottos cause at night.

### The Crowned Eagle

Naturally, the Diana monkey and other friendly monkeys are not alone in the high trees. Many other animals share their rain forest environment. Some of them are the monkeys' enemies. One typical enemy is the crowned eagle, a bird of prey. Monkeys are fearful of this large, powerful African eagle with good reason. The crowned eagle hunts tree monkeys.

Only a few observers have actually seen Diana monkeys being alarmed by predators. Generally, their enemies hunt at night. But they become very alarmed when a crowned eagle flies above the tree canopy. A single cry signals the group that an eagle is near. The alarm is sounded by the females who make a short, loud call. The call sounds as if they are saying "K9." All members of the group, both young and old, respond quickly by climbing down from high branches.

The two animals that monkeys fear most are the eagle and the leopard. The warning signal that monkeys use is different for each animal. If the predator is an eagle, the group scrambles down the tree after hearing the warning call. If the enemy is a leopard, they know by the alarm cry that they must escape to higher branches.

By using tree monkeys as its main food, the eagle has a

The tree monkeys fear the leopard and the crowned eagle more than any other animals of the forest. They alert one another to the presence of these predators using different cries of alarm. If a leopard *(above left)* approaches, the monkeys' cry tells others to escape to high, inaccessible branches. If the feared terrible crowned eagle *(above right)* is spotted, the signal tells the clan to head toward the ground. Monkeys also scream to drive off their enemies. For example, when they discover an eagle or leopard in their resting places, they boldly surround the intruder. They scream so wildly that all animals in the forest nearby are disturbed. Eventually, the intruder leaves.

In this diagram, the wingspan of the crowned eagle is compared with that of Verreaux's eagle. The crowned eagle, with its shorter, broader, rounded wings and longer tail, is better adapted to living in the forest. The Verreaux's eagle typically lives in open spaces. Because of these physical differences, the crowned eagle is expert at swooping in and out among the branches of the forest. It also plunges quickly downward to capture its prey.

Verreaux's eagle

crowned eagle

plentiful food supply. The upper tree level is home to many colobus monkeys, guenons, black-and-white colobus monkeys, mangabeys, and pottos. It is no wonder that these powerful winged predators specialize in hunting these animals.

In other tropical forests, different species of birds of prey occupy the same ecological niche as the crowned eagle occupies in Africa. Two examples are the monkey-eating eagle in the Philippines and the harpy eagle in South America. These birds are similar to the crowned eagle in size, appearance, and behavior. All three birds share the same food preference.

Eagles have some powerful weapons. With their long, sharp claws, eagles grasp a monkey's head and quickly crush the skull. The eagle's strategy is to kill a monkey instantly. This is important for the eagle's own safety. If the monkey fought back, it would have both its hands and feet with which to fight. With them, it could tear the feathers of its attacker. The eagle would probably win the battle, but it might come away injured or without important feathers. Its ability to hunt might be impaired. Eventually, its life would be in danger.

The crowned eagle constantly patrols the huge canopy of the tropical forest. Sometimes it travels in a pair, but more often it is alone. It flies slowly and silently, often circling the tallest trees that rise above the canopy. As soon as it spots its prey, it plunges into the dense foliage. It attacks with amazing accuracy. It is so agile that it can swoop among branches and trunks to chase a victim. Sometimes, it dives rapidly and catches its prey far below on the ground. If the prey is very large, the eagle leaves the trees. It carries its prey to the ground and feeds on it there.

Crowned eagle nests are found high in the treetops. They are built as high as 110 to 130 feet (30 to 40 m) above the ground. Generally, the eagles build them in large forks in trees. The nest is made of a large bunch of branches. Eagles that return to the same nest year after year continue bringing branches. Eventually, the nest is so enormous that it can be seen from quite a distance. In it, the eagle lays two eggs. After hatching, the stronger chick generally kills the weaker one. One is left to grow to maturity.

The young stay in the nest for a very long time. An eaglet continues to be fed by its parents once or twice a day until it is six or seven months old. After it begins to fly, the young bird still returns to the nest to be fed. The eagle must

The mustached guenon gets its name from the white, mustachelike stripe on its nose. This mark makes the monkey easy to distinguish from other tree monkeys. This species lives in forests from Cameroon to the Congo. It feeds mainly on oil palm seeds and occupies roughly the same area as its food supply.

be a very skilled hunter to survive in the dense tropical forest. For this reason, the young eagle may stay with its parents a long time. In the nest, the young bird will learn its parents' methods of surviving in the complex forest environment.

## The Companions of the Guenons

A variety of animals make their homes near the monkeys and the eagles. One species, the Diana monkey, may see dozens of other species each day of its life. Researchers have reported seeing as many as seventy-six species of birds in the guenons' territory. To better understand the variety of animal life, scientists studied a small area of about 4 sq. miles (10 sq. km). There they found more than thirty species of medium-sized mammals. They also found an equal number of small mammals. These included animals such as rats, mice, shrews, weasels, skunks, and badgers.

*Right:* Demidoff's bush baby and its relative, the eastern needle-clawed bush baby, are varieties of galagos. These monkeys are widespread in Africa's forests. Bush babies are lively and agile little animals. They have adapted well to living in trees. Having long legs, they make excellent jumpers. Their long, furry tails help their balance. They use their tails like parachutes when they drop from high branches to lower levels. Their fingers and toes have flat disks of thickened skin. This feature helps them grasp slippery branches and helps them perform acrobatics in trees.

*Opposite:* An adult potto leaves its baby sleeping and sets off to search for food. When these animals sleep, they hang from branches, rolled up like a ball. Pottos belong to the Lorisidae family. Galagos and Lorisidae family members are types of early (less evolved) monkeys called prosimians.

Of course, more monkey species were also found. There were black-and-white colobus monkeys, red colobus monkeys, Congo white-nosed guenons, and mangabeys. They also noted the presence of the small, tree-dwelling potto, Demidoff's bush babies, and eastern needle-clawed bush babies. These last three species are early primates, or prosimians. They have long tails and large eyes that are well adapted to darkness.

The potto is a nocturnal animal. A nocturnal animal is active at night. The potto sleeps all day, hanging from tree branches with its head between its arms. In this position, it seems to be nothing more than a large ball of fur. At night-fall, it becomes an alert predator. It hunts small animals and forages for fruit and leaves.

Bush babies get their name from the sound they make. When they call out, it sounds as if babies are crying in the forest. A Demidoff's bush baby is about 6 inches (14 cm) long. The larger eastern needle-clawed bush baby grows to a length of 8 inches (20 cm) or more. They both have long, thick tails and are graceful jumpers. When they leap toward a distant trunk, they seem to be flying. Bush babies are adaptable animals. They make their home in all wooded areas. They live in rain forests, secondary forests, and the woods of savannahs. They are omnivorous, which means they eat both plant and animal matter. Bush babies commonly eat animals such as young birds, lizards, and small rodents. They also eat plants such as nuts and fruit.

49

# CHIMPANZEES AND GORILLAS

Chimpanzees and gorillas are two of the most popular zoo attractions. In the wild, they make their homes in the equatorial forest. Perhaps it is because they so closely resemble humans that people find them so fascinating. Actually, both humans and monkeys belong to the same biological order. This order is known as the primates. The gorilla is the largest and most advanced animal of the African tropical forest. By nature, it is shy and gentle. Both chimpanzees and gorillas are known to be gregarious, spending their lives in groups. These groups are territorial and mark certain forest regions as their own.

The chimpanzee is the tree-dweller. It spends its days in the branches and builds its sleeping nests there. The gorilla lives on the forest floor. It has little to fear, even from large predators such as the leopard. With its strength, large size, and the support of its group, a gorilla has little trouble defending itself.

Various monkey species live on different forest levels. In charting the different species' living space, a pattern develops. The least advanced monkey groups live at the highest level. The most advanced groups live at the lowest. High in the canopy are the small, agile guenons. The guenons are the least developed of the forest primates. More advanced groups such as colobus monkeys and mangabeys occupy the middle level of trees. Finally, the most advanced monkeys are found close to or on the ground. Of course, these are the chimpanzees and gorillas.

Nocturnal tree monkeys like galagos and pottos are also found in the canopy level. Nearer to the ground are the mandrills and drills. These monkeys are similar except for their noses. Mandrills have red noses, drills have black noses. Mandrills are a species of monkey that returned from the savannah to the forest. They spend their time on the ground and in the lower trees. Finally, at the ground level are baboons.

## Primate Relatives

The great apes originated in Africa during the Tertiary period, 30 to 35 million years ago. As the great tropical rain forest evolved through the ages, so did primates. Fossil remains of *Proconsul*, a small humanlike creature, were found in East Africa. Scientists estimate it lived a little less than thirty million years ago. But strangely, this ancient creature did not adapt to forest life, the habitat of present-day apes. From Africa, this early human went to ancient

*Opposite:* A young gorilla is seen in the forest of Bukavu, Zaire, while feeding on shoots. The African equatorial forest is home to three species of anthropoid, or humanlike apes: the gorilla, the chimpanzee, and the dwarf chimpanzee. However, the three groups occupy different ecological niches in the forest. Small groups of gorillas live on the ground and only use the lower branches of trees when resting. Chimpanzees occupy the foliage level immediately above. They are only occasionally found on the ground. Dwarf chimpanzees, the smallest apes, live at the highest tree level.

Asia. There it learned to live in the trees.

People came later. That story also begins in the heart of Africa. In fact, about two million years ago, ancient *hominids* populated the entire African continent. These early human beings were called "australopithecines."

Apes such as chimpanzees and gorillas are known as anthropoid because they resemble humans. This similarity goes deeper than its appearance. Apes have the same blood composition as humans. Therefore, the two are blood relatives. Recent scientific studies show that the dwarf chimpanzee's blood resembles human blood more than it resembles blood of the common chimpanzee. Scientists also have learned that humans share a tropical ancestry with the gorilla. They also share ancestry with the orangutan. This ape lives in the Asian islands of Sumatra and Borneo. In short, anthropoid apes represent a wild, tree-dwelling time of human evolution.

## Chimpanzees

The chimpanzee is probably the most popular of all the great apes. Scientists have studied it intensely. They have

observed it both inside and outside its natural habitat. The chimpanzee belongs to a genus that is found only in Africa. The genus has only two species, the chimpanzee and the dwarf chimpanzee, or bonobo.

Today, the territory of the common chimpanzee is in the tropical areas of eastern central Africa. The area includes parts of Senegal, Nigeria, Cameroon, Sudan, and Tanzania up to Lake Tanganyika. Once the chimpanzee was very common throughout this region. Today, it no longer exists in numerous areas of West Africa between Senegal and the Ivory Coast. In the eastern areas, the chimpanzee's survival is threatened. Much forest land is being used for plantations, logging, or homes. As this happens, the chimpanzee's habitat grows smaller. Some chimpanzees are captured and used for commercial purposes, such as circuses. Today, the chimpanzee is a species in grave risk of extinction. It is now included on the red list of endangered species of the International Union for Nature Conservation.

The dwarf chimpanzee is also called the "bonobo." It very closely resembles the common chimpanzee, but it is smaller and more slender. Its legs and arms also are longer compared to its smaller body. Its fur is dark brown. Unlike many mammals, this chimpanzee has no sagittal crest, the bony ridge on top of the skull. It is not found over as wide a range as the common chimpanzee. It dwells mostly in primary and secondary tropical forests. Until recently, the dwarf chimpanzee was a rather common species. Now it is very rare. Today, it is found in the southern part of Zaire's Congo River basin and in the central Congo.

Scientists have not done extensive study on the dwarf chimpanzee in its natural habitat. This is due, in part, to the location of the chimpanzee's habitat. This species commonly dwells in the canopy as high up as 100 to 150 feet (30 to 50 m). There it feeds on fruit and leaves. Dwarf chimpanzees live in groups and have a complex social life. They build sleeping nests at heights of about 50 feet (15 m) from the ground. This is higher than where common chimpanzees build their nests. They build nests about 16 to 65 feet (5 to 20 m) from the ground. However, both types of chimpanzees will drop to the cooler ground level during the hot afternoon hours.

The chimpanzee has been the object of much attention by zoologists and ethologists. These two types of scientists study animal behavior. They are particularly interested in how chimpanzees think, learn, and relate to other chimpan-

*Opposite:* The agile chimpanzee can move easily through tree branches and on the ground. Well-worn paths *(shown in the picture)* mark their travels. As chimpanzees move, they use different gaits and stand in different positions. The drawing illustrates different positions of movement. When moving slowly, the chimpanzee walks on four legs. Its weight is on the knuckles of its hands, and its feet are flat on the ground. When moving faster, the chimpanzee uses its toes only. When running, the chimpanzee stands partially erect and swings its arms. The chimpanzee's fastest run is a kind of gallop. During this gallop, it throws its arms and legs forward in quick succession. When standing as erect as possible, the chimpanzee can only move very slowly. It seldom stays in this position for long.

*Below:* Chimpanzees are among the few animals capable of using real tools. Generally, the tools are used to obtain food. For example, chimpanzees use special twigs to dig into termites' mounds. These twigs are kept for later use.

zees. By studying this species, ethologists can learn important information about human behavior and development. Because chimpanzees are human's closest relative, they are used for many scientific research projects.

The chimpanzee lives mainly in tropical rain forests. But it also lives in gallery forests. These forests also are called tunnel forests because they grow along both sides of some rivers. Chimpanzees also live in mountain forests up to about 10,000 feet (3,000 m). Their habitat does not overlap with that of the gorilla. The gorilla usually lives at lower altitudes.

Chimpanzees that live in the savannah do not behave the same as forest chimpanzees. An American ethologist, Jane Goodall, spent several years studying chimpanzees of the savannah woodlands. Her studies were conducted in the Gombe Game Reserve in Tanzania. There she was able to observe chimpanzees in the wild. Eventually, Goodall's group of chimpanzees accepted her as a member.

Troops of chimpanzees claim territories of different size. A territory's size depends on the amount of available ripe fruit, leaves, and roots. The Budongo Forest in Uganda is very fertile. Each troop there needs only about 8 sq. miles (20 sq. km) to satisfy its food needs. On the other hand, in the Gombe, food is not so plentiful. There, each group needs a territory as large as 15 to 23 sq. miles (40 to 60 sq. km).

Chimpanzees are typically gregarious animals. They live in troops of up to fifty or sixty members. In the forest, troop composition varies. One troop may have several males and females. Or it may have only males or only females with young and infants. Sometimes, individual males are found living alone in the forest. Often members of one group wander off and join other groups.

Chimpanzees and other large animals use well-worn paths as they travel through their territories. Sometimes, two troops meet on a path. Generally, they do not try to drive one another from the territory. Instead, the two groups mix in a friendly way for a while before continuing on their way.

## Daily Life of the Chimpanzees

The chimpanzee's day starts at dawn. Troop members leave their nests to feed on leaves and fruit found in the resting area. Later, they head to other locations where a variety of food is available. There they feed undisturbed. Generally, they search for different species of trees with ripe fruit, young leaves, and roots.

The greatest enemies of the chimpanzee are human beings and leopards. When a person approaches its habitat, the chimpanzee becomes silent and quickly flees. However, if a leopard intrudes in its territory, the chimpanzee and the rest of its troop form a semicircle around the predator. They display their characteristic threat posture—chin jutting out, arms open, and fur raised. (This is shown by the chimpanzee in the background of the drawing.) Other chimpanzees drive off the leopard with uprooted bushes and torn branches.

Observations of wild chimpanzees made by Jane Goodall and others show that they use tools. Often they use tools to obtain food in hard-to-reach locations. For example, they gather small sticks and carefully shape them. With the sticks, they dig into termite mounds, ant hills, or bee hives. Then they pull them out and lick off the small insects or honey. Chimpanzees also use leaves as tools. Shredding green or dry leaves, they mold them with their hands into a spongelike mass. Then they put the leaves in hard-to-reach places where water collects, such as holes in trees. When the leaves absorb the water, the chimpanzees retrieve them. Squeezing the leave-mass, they drink the water that drips out.

An unusual behavior is the chimpanzee's habit of using plants as appetizers. Some chimpanzees chew but do not swallow certain plant leaves before a meal.

After the main meal, the group rests for several hours. Often they rest in nests on the ground or in trees. These nests are only temporary. Chimpanzees build them in a few minutes by bending and weaving branches and twigs. At this time, members of the troop interact with one another socially. Youngsters play while others groom one another. Chimpanzees spend a considerable amount of time grooming themselves and each other. They go through fur, picking out dirt, burrs, dried skin, ticks, and splinters. The last part of the day is spent in a final feeding. After the brilliant tropical sunset, the whole troop settles down. They sleep on sturdier nests that are used for several nights. These sleeping nests are built high in the trees from 20 to 65 feet (6 to 20 m) off the ground.

Aside from people, the only natural enemy of this species is the leopard. Chimpanzees use their great numbers to fight against this predator. As soon as they know that a leopard is near, chimpanzees become very aggressive. They threaten the enemy with raised arms and jutting chins. Their fur even stands on end. At once, some of the chimpanzees form a semicircle around the leopard. They hurl branches and bushes at it. At the same time, adult males form another group and attack the leopard with sticks.

Chimpanzees respond very differently when approached by people. One of the troop warns the group with a short cry. The group becomes silent and motionless. If they sense that the person has seen them, they drop to the ground quietly and flee.

Generally, chimpanzees are vegetarians. Scientists have

A female mountain gorilla is pictured with her infant. This species of gorilla is on the endangered list. Its habitat is shrinking as more people use the forest land. Mountain gorillas now number only about a thousand. They are found only in the mountain forests that lie between Rwanda, Zaire, and Uganda at about 10,000 to 13,000 feet (3,000 to 4,000 m) high. Many areas in this region have been set aside as reserves for the protection of the mountain gorilla

identified over eighty species of plants in the equatorial forest that chimpanzees like to eat. From them they gather ripe fruit, leaves, flowers, roots, bark, and seeds. Even hard-shelled fruit or nuts are no obstacle for this primate. To get at the tasty pulp or nutmeat, they beat hard shells against a tree trunk or with a stick.

Chimpanzees are interested in most food sources. Sometimes they eat termites, ants, and insect larvae. At times, they also prey on small vertebrates (animals with backbones). The chimpanzees sometimes eat such animals as young forest antelope. They may even eat young monkeys, such as colobus monkeys or baboons. After capturing a small monkey, the chimpanzee kills it by grabbing its hind legs. It then beats the monkey on the ground or against a tree trunk. After the kill, the chimpanzee divides its prey equally among members of the group.

## Gorillas

In the past, movies portrayed the gorilla as a fierce and dangerous monster. It now has a much better image. Today, most people know that the gorilla is a large, gentle, herbi-

The silvery white back of this splendid male gorilla is a sign of its dominant position in the group. No more than three or four dominant males live in each gorilla troop. One holds the position of leader, and each male beneath him has a special rank.

vorous ape. It has strong social ties with other members of its group. Unfortunately, its peaceful nature makes it an easy target for hunters. Natives often kill gorillas for food. Gorillas also are killed by poachers—people who kill or capture animals illegally. Other gorillas are killed by growers who are protecting their crops. Still others are dying out because their forest habitat is being destroyed.

Since 1933, international laws have forbidden the hunting of gorillas. But the laws have not been successful in preserving this magnificent ape. Today, the gorilla is an endangered species. Human use of the forest has increased in the area where gorillas make their homes. Only one

thousand mountain gorillas, a subspecies, remain. They live in the mountain forests between Zaire, Uganda and Rwanda. They live nowhere else in the world. Two other subspecies remain. They are the western lowland gorilla and the eastern lowland gorilla. The western lowland gorilla lives in the tropical rain forests of Congo, Gabon, and equatorial Guinea. The eastern lowland gorilla lives in the eastern Congo extending to the Central African Lakes region. Their habitats are similar. But together, these lowland gorillas only number a few thousand.

Despite their reputations as ferocious animals, gorillas are the most gentle and tolerant of all apes. They have peaceful relationships with members of their own group. They also live peacefully with similar species that wander into their territory. The territory, in fact, varies according to the size of the group. It may cover 4 to 15 sq. miles (10 to 40 sq. km). Unlike the arboreal monkeys which drive off intruders, gorillas do not defend their territory very strongly. In fact, when two groups of gorillas meet, they behave in a friendly manner. They mix together and share various activities. After a few hours, they set off again, going their separate ways into the forest. It seems that gorilla territories are shared equally by all gorillas that live in a large region. This behavior is unique among apes.

Until about thirty years ago, not much was known about the gorilla. Thanks to the work of zoologists George Schaller and Diane Fossey, this is no longer the case. Reliable information about the biology and behavior of this large primate is now available. George Schaller began to study gorillas in 1959. Diane Fossey spent thirteen years with the gorillas between 1967 and 1980. One gorilla group eventually accepted her. She was then able to closely observe gorilla behavior. From this work, she gathered an extraordinary amount of information.

## The Social Behavior of Gorillas

Large adult males have black fur with silvery white backs. Each has a bony crest on the top of its skull. This gives a helmetlike effect to the head. The males are huge, powerful animals. They weigh as much as 550 pounds (250 kg). Males dominate the group, although they never use violence to rule the others. The elder leader is usually a gentle ruler. He only needs to gesture or change his expression to get his way. A male does not attain a higher position or rank by defeating others in battles. He attains position

The drawing shows a troop of gorillas during a rest period. *Left to right:* A young gorilla rests; a male rests in a fork of a tree; young gorillas play; a female carries her infant; the male leader beats his chest in a threatening display.

by quietly intimidating others. Gorillas are often pictured threatening one another by standing on their hind legs and beating their chests. Actually this is rarely seen.

Social groups generally consist of a few family members. Mountain gorillas may have troops with as many as twenty members. A troop usually includes two or more males. The lowland gorillas, however, travel in smaller troops. For example, in Cameroon, a lowland gorilla troop may consist of a male, a female, and one to three young. In Zaire, one troop may have one male and two or three females with young.

Gorillas spend most of their time on the ground. They inhabit the trees less than any other ape. On the ground, they are almost continually on the move. They walk in single file, guided by the leader. They live in a nomadic way in order to use food sources evenly in their territory.

Each day at dusk, these ground-dwellers build sleeping nests. They fold branches and young trees and stuff them

with grass and ferns. Adult males always sleep on the ground. Females and young sleep in nests in the trees.

Gorillas follow a peaceful daily routine. They leave their nests between six and eight in the morning. They then spend two or three hours feeding. The gorilla's diet is varied, but completely vegetarian. It includes over one hundred plant species. Plant leaves are a major part of the diet. But gorillas also feed on shoots, roots, bark, and tubers. When possible, they invade plantations. There they eat cultivated fruit and plants, such as bananas and sugar cane. These raids can cause considerable damage. Because of their size, the gorillas eat great amounts of food. Finally, during the hottest hours of the day, the gorillas rest lazily. Late in the afternoon, they start to feed again or move to other areas.

Studies such as those of Schaller and Fossey have changed people's minds about the gorilla. It is no longer thought of as the dangerous, ferocious humanlike forest ape. Instead, it is now seen as a kind of friendly giant.

# UNGULATES

Far below the level where tree monkeys romp, animals known as "ungulates" roam the equatorial forest. Ungulates are animals that have hooves. Much was learned about ungulates while studying blue monkeys in the Kibale Forest. The most typical ungulates in the forest are forest antelope and Old World pigs. Ungulates' bodies are more suited for life in the open savannah than to life in the forest. They are found in greater number in the savannah. Nevertheless, many species of ungulates still live in the African equatorial forest. The most common are the bushbuck, the blue duiker, Harvey's duiker, the bush pig, the warthog, the giant forest pig, and the dwarf buffalo.

## Forest Antelope

Most scientists agree that the antelope of today were originally ancient savannah species. The species spread to the forest environment. Because of this change in habitat, the antelope's body eventually changed. It adapted to the new environment in several ways. First, the forest antelope grew smaller in size. This allowed it to move through the dense foliage and trees. Today, some species of dwarf antelope are the size of a hare. Second, forest antelope developed stockier bodies. Third, their cumbersome horns became smaller and simpler. Fourth, they began to live alone. Before this, antelope had lived in herds. Living in a herd had advantages in the savannah. There greater numbers were needed to watch open areas for predators. This strategy is not useful in the dense forest. So, to adapt, the antelope learned to live alone.

Duikers are the most typical small antelope. The giant duiker weighs about 143 pounds (65 kg), while the small blue duiker weighs about 26 pounds (12 kg). In all, there are about fifteen species of duiker, including the banded duiker and the red duiker. These shy animals have adapted so well to the forest that they are difficult to study. Their small, swept-back horns do not catch the foliage. Their dark coat is difficult to detect in the shadowy woods. Some species, such as the banded duiker, are camouflaged by vertical, black stripes along their backs and sides. Other forest herbivores such as the bongo and the okapi have this zebralike coloration. This color pattern confuses predators. It is difficult enough seeing an animal body against the forest background. Between the shafts of light and shadow, the duiker's striped body is even more difficult to see.

In the forest, duikers have their own territories. They

*Opposite:* The bush pig is an Old World pig of average size. Along with many subspecies, the bush pig ranges from the southern Sahara Desert to South Africa and Madagascar. This pig is active at night. It lives in family herds that usually number about ten. At times, the herd may number in the hundreds. The bush pig's diet includes mostly grass, fruit, roots, and very rarely, small animals.

The body structure of small forest antelope evolved from the need to move about easily in wooded areas. As a result, duikers have small, straight horns which do not get caught in underbrush. They have rounded bodies with legs that slope inward and curved rumps which help them dart for cover in thick underbrush.

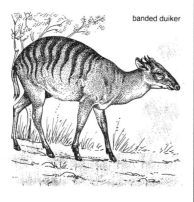

banded duiker

red duiker

giant duiker

defend these territories from intruders. Duikers mark their area with secretions from special glands in their snouts. Then they recognize the territory by its smell. Duikers use special sections of their territories for different activities. They rest in one section and feed in another. Paths that connect these areas are easy to spot.

Duikers have a strange diet. They are the only ruminants, or grazing animals, that also eat other animals. They behave as predators. Generally, termites are their only prey,

The blue duiker is the smallest of the forest antelope. In fact, it does not grow larger than 20 inches (50 cm) high. It does not weigh more than 26 pounds (12 kg). Like others of its genus, it comes out of the forest at nightfall and feeds in clearings. There it becomes easy prey for the leopard, python, and crowned eagle. Its main defense is its coloring which blends in well with its surroundings.

but they have been known to rob bird nests. In captivity, they also kill and devour pigeons and chickens. Generally, forest antelope mainly eat grasses, leaves, and shoots. Sometimes they follow troops of colobus monkeys and guenons. They hope to find fruit that these messy eaters drop while feeding high up in the canopy.

## Dwarf Antelope

The small body size of forest ungulates is an adaptation that allows them to move easily through dense forest. Dwarf antelope and dik-diks are examples of this type of evolution. The smallest antelope in the world is the royal antelope. The antelope gets its name from an African expression meaning "king of the hares." This dwarf antelope is the smallest living bovid. It is a ruminant like oxen, sheep, goats, and true antelope. In spite of its regal name, the royal antelope is a tiny animal. It measures about 15 inches (40 cm) long and 10 inches (25 cm) high. It weighs about 4 pounds (2 kg). It has thin legs and a rounded back. Its reddish brown coat becomes white on the stomach. The male has two little horns that are about 1.5 inches (3.5 cm) long. This unique animal is found only in Sierra Leone, the Ivory Coast, and Ghana. Two other species of dwarf antelope, Bates' dwarf antelope and the suni, are slightly larger.

Dwarf antelope are not found only in the tropical rain forest. They also inhabit other forests such as tunnel forests and areas where scrub vegetation and bush grow. They can survive in both humid and dry climates up to altitudes of about 6,500 feet (2,000 m) above sea level. These small animals are nocturnal. Like larger ungulates, they mark off their own territories. Though they usually live alone or in pairs, they are sometimes seen in herds when grazing in open land.

Dik-diks belong to the genus *Madoqua* and are small antelope that only grow to the size of a hare. Unlike the dwarf antelope of the forest, dik-diks dwell in the savannah woodland.

## Bushbucks and Bongos

Two of the larger forest antelope are bushbucks and bongos. Bushbucks grow to a length of about 5 feet (1.5 m) and a height of about 3 feet (1 m). Their lyre-shaped horns measure about 21 inches (55 cm). Each bushbuck occupies a territory about one-tenth of a square mile (.30 sq km). Each marks it by scent or by "scoring" trees with its horns. They

A female bushbuck and her offspring stop at a watering place. Along with the bongo, the bushbuck is the largest antelope of the African forest. Like almost all of the inhabitants of the woods, it is solitary and territorial. It lives in areas where the foliage is less dense.

are the only antelope of the genus *Tragelaphus* found in the virgin tropical forest. They are the only ones that live alone. Others of this genus, such as the kudu, nyala, and the sitatunga, are herbivores and live in the savannah.

Bushbucks are widespread throughout southern Africa. They exist from the tropical forests at the southern border of the Sahara Desert to Cape Province of South Africa. They inhabit highlands up to about 13,000 feet (4,000 m) above sea level. They have brown fur, though the shade and markings differ. In Kenya, for example, bushbucks have dark brown coats. But in Cameroon, they are golden brown with white spots and stripes running up and down.

The largest forest antelope is the bongo. It weighs 485 pounds (220 kg) and is 9 feet (2.8 m) long. Both the male and female have lyre-shaped horns that grow to a length of about 3 feet (1 m). Their dark coats are crossed by narrow white stripes. This species is found in the tropical rain forests from Sierra Leone to Tanzania except for Dahomey and Nigeria. This antelope never strays far from water. It seeks out the dense, wet bamboo forests during the heat of the day. Like its smaller forest relatives, it lives alone. It is territorial except during times of drought when it moves on to find suitable grazing. Bongos are well known for their beautiful coats.

# ZOOLOGICAL DISCOVERIES OF THE TWENTIETH CENTURY

Of all the ecosystems on this planet, the tropical forest is truly the most preserved. Its main characteristics have remained unchanged for millions of years. In a sense, it is a vast plant museum. Although they have survived longer than any other plant collection on earth, tropical forests are the last to be studied. This is because they are so difficult to explore. As recently as the beginning of this century, some large and very interesting animals that live in these forests were still unknown.

Three new animal species were discovered when the last virgin areas of equatorial Africa were explored. One of them was the okapi. The okapi is the only living relative of the giraffe. Another recent discovery was an Old World pig. This animal, now known as the giant forest pig, lives its entire life in the forest. The Congo peafowl was also found. Scientists think that this peafowl is related to large Asian land birds such as the pheasant, turkey, and grouse. They are particularly interested in the peafowl because it survived long after similar species died out. Plants and animals such as the peafowl that survive from an earlier period are called "relics."

All three animals were discovered and scientifically investigated. The research was a long and difficult job. Scientists were aided by accidental discoveries such as skin fragments and strange feathers in out-of-the-way places. Some clues that these animals existed came from dusty storerooms of large European and American museums. In time, the researchers were able to identify the animals. The okapi was described in 1901. The giant forest pig was described in 1904. The Congo peafowl was identified around 1930.

## The Okapi

At one time, a fish known as the coelacanth (*Latimeria chalumnae*) was thought to be extinct. Scientists knew that it once existed because they found fossil remains in waters near South Africa. Later they learned that living specimens of the coelacanth were found in South African waters.

The story of the okapi's discovery is similar. About ten million years ago, a herbivore known by the scientific name *Helladotherium* lived in Europe and Asia. By 1900, scientists knew much about this animal because they found many fossil remains. They described this ancient animal as a member of the giraffe family. Its neck and legs, however, were shorter than those of the modern giraffe. In 1901,

*Opposite:* The okapi is a large forest ungulate, or hooved animal. It is the only living relative of the giraffe. This strange animal was only recently discovered because its habitat is very dense and impenetrable. Its range is in the Ituri Forest between Zaire and Uganda. This is considered the heart of the central African equatorial forest.

scientists in London examined okapi skulls for the first time. They found that the modern skulls were very similar to those of the animal thought to be extinct.

News of this okapi was first heard in 1880. At that time, the British explorer, Sir Henry Stanley, was traveling in an unexplored Congo forest. From pygmies there, he heard of a horselike animal in the deep forest. Stanley knew that horses usually live in the steppe and savannah. He wondered how they could live in the heart of the great tropical forest. In 1900, scientists obtained the first evidence of this strange animal. The governor of Uganda, a man named Johnston, sent two fragments of skin to the Royal Zoological Society. The mysterious "horse" was named "Johnston's horse," until more could be learned about the animal.

The following year, the scientists received an entire skin and two skulls for examination. They found that the animal was not related to horses, mules, or antelope. Instead, it was a member of the giraffe family. The okapi turned out to be the only living relative of the true giraffe. The new species was called "Johnston's okapi," or *Okapia johnstoni*. It was really a very ancient species.

The okapi is a strange and interesting mammal that has some fascinating traits. It has a large body structure, measuring over 5 feet (1.7 m) high at the "withers." An animal's withers refers to the highest point of its back. It is also about 7 feet ( 2.1 m) long and can weigh over 550 pounds (250 kg). In general, it resembles a horse with a reddish brown coat. Its hindquarters and forelegs are covered with large, uneven black-and-white stripes. The okapi is also known for its unusual tongue. The tongue is very long and functions like an elephant's trunk. It makes it easy for the okapi to gather leaves, twigs, and fruit on which it feeds.

Like all forest species, the okapi is very difficult to study. Little is known about its behavior. Its diet is mainly vegetarian, consisting of leaves, tender twigs, fruit, and shoots. In clearings, it finds grasses, ferns, and mushrooms. Sometimes it eats cultivated plants such as cassava and sweet potato. A strange part of its diet is spurges, a plant that is very poisonous to both people and other animals.

The okapis prefer dry, dense forest areas where they live alone. They pair only long enough to mate. They are territorial and defend their own regions. At most, one okapi occupies about one-third of a square mile (1 sq. km). Its only predator other than people is the leopard. But young okapi are also prey for the African golden cat and the serval. The

Opposite: Little is known about the okapi's habits and behavior because it lives in such remote areas. Most studies have been conducted on okapis in captivity. The drawings show how the male teaches and plays with his male offspring. *Top to bottom:* The young nuzzles its father, provoking him to fight. Next, the young male threatens the adult by thrusting its muzzle into the air. The young starts to fight by whipping its neck against the adult's neck, just as an adult would battle. After a while, the father pretends to be defeated and lies on the ground in a submissive posture. Finally, the proud young okapi displays the typical threat posture. All of the threat postures shown are typical of the adult okapi.

*Below:* The giant forest pig, which looks like a wild boar, is the largest living Old World pig. Because of its strength and ability to use its pointed, protruding lower teeth as weapons, this pig does not fear predators.

okapi has a habit of using the same paths over and over again. By following these paths, pygmies hunt okapis without much difficulty. To trap them, the natives build pits that are about 7 feet (2 m) deep. The pit has smooth sides and a narrow bottom. The opening is covered with branches. Antelope and duikers are agile enough to jump out of these traps. The okapi is not so lucky. Its body structure does not allow it to stand on its hind legs or jump from the pit. The trapped okapi is easily captured and killed.

## The Giant Forest Pig

Tropical forests grow in two large areas of the world. Scientists call these areas the New World, or American tropics, and the Old World tropics. These divisions help when identifying forests and the plants and animals in them.

The Old World pig is also known as the giant forest pig. It lives strictly in the tropical forest. As with the okapi, local natives first told outsiders of the existence of this species. In 1900, these stories aroused the curiosity of English lieutenant Richard Meinertzhagen. He began searching for this

A thick rain forest, as shown here, covers southern Nigeria. The dense and often impenetrable tropical forest makes travel difficult. But it is an ideal environment for camouflaging wildlife. Many animals species living in this environment (such as the okapi, the giant forest pig, and the Congo peafowl) were unknown to scientists until this century. The forests are still some of the least-explored environments on earth. It is probable that new discoveries await zoologists who study this land in the future.

unusual species. While in Kenya in 1904, he obtained the skull and hide of the giant pig. Two years later, skull parts of the same species were also found in the Congo. Only then did the giant forest pig officially become part of the fauna of the African tropical forest. This find was important because the Old World pig is one of the largest African mammals. It measures about 6 feet (1.8 m) long and 3 feet (1 m) high at the shoulder. It weighs up to 660 pounds (300 kg).

The giant forest pig resembles a large boar. It has a brown or black coat and ash gray skin. It uses its large teeth to attack other animals and to defend itself. Its upper side teeth curve inward and may be as long as 12 inches (30 cm). Its short, wide lower teeth protrude outward.

Usually forest pigs of the eastern regions are larger than those that inhabit western regions. Giant forest pigs roam over fairly large territories. They travel in social groups that consist of four to twelve members. Generally, a male, female, a few juveniles, and young travel together. Occasionally, males travel alone. A group uses the thickest vegetation in its territory as a daytime resting spot. At night, it moves to feeding areas and searches for food.

Because they are large animals and fierce fighters, Old World pigs have little to fear from predators. Adults are so quick to defend their offspring that even the leopard will not prey on the young.

Like many other forest animals, the behavior and daily habits of the giant forest pig have not been studied in depth. For one thing, this animal is difficult to track in the wild. As well, it often changes its location within its territory.

## The Congo Peafowl

The discovery of the Congo peafowl was very interesting. First, scientists were amazed to find a new species as late as the twentieth century. Secondly, this bird proved that land birds of Africa and Asia were related. In fact, scientists found that the peafowl's closest relatives inhabit areas far from the Congo. One relative is the common peafowl of India. Another is the helmeted guinea fowl of southern Africa.

The male peafowl is known as the peacock and the female is a peahen. The male and female both have partially bare necks and showy crests of white feathers on their heads. The Congo peafowl of Africa lives in humid tropical forests. It is the largest forest bird in Africa. Although it flies occasionally, most of its life is spent on the ground.

*Opposite:* The Congo peafowl is a large land bird of the forest. It was described for the first time in 1934. It is only found in one area (shown by the shaded area on the map) in the eastern basin of the Congo River. It is particularly interesting to zoologists. They believe that it represents a link between the Asian common peafowl and the African helmeted guineafowl. Although its colors are somewhat bright, the Congo peafowl does not have the spectacular large tail which common peacocks fan out during mating displays. Instead, it merely circles the female with wings open and the tail raised *(bottom)*.

74

Range of the
Congo peafowl

An ornithologist's keen powers of observation led to the peafowl's discovery. The ornithologist, an American named James Chapin, was on an expedition in Zaire's Ituri Forest. Stopping at the village of Arakubi, he saw unusual bird feathers in the tribal chief's headdress. When he returned to New York, Chapin took some of the mysterious feathers with him. He hoped to trace the bird's identity at the New York Museum of Natural History. In spite of his research, he failed to match them with any known African species.

Twenty years later in 1934, Chapin was in Belgium studying African animal life at the Belgian Congo Museum. By chance, he went into one of the museum's storage rooms. In a dark hallway, he came across two stuffed birds that he had never seen before. They were simply classified as "young peacocks," probably an Indian species. Examining them carefully, Chapin decided that the classification was wrong. Their unusual colors were not typical of the Indian peafowl. One was dark blue-black. It had long, strong spurs, which the Indian species seldom has. The other was reddish brown. But the feathers were familiar to Chapin. They reminded him of the feathers he had seen in Zaire but had not been able to identify. He quickly wrote to New York and had the mysterious African feathers sent to him. He then compared them to those in the museum. He found that the secondary flight feathers of the reddish specimen matched his African feathers in color and size. Eventually, he proved that the stuffed bird in the museum was actually a species that scientists had never identified before. He had discovered *Afropavas congensis*, the Congo peafowl.

This large bird lives strictly in the forest and only in the eastern basin of the Congo River. It occupies hilly areas or environments where flooding does not occur. It is omnivorous. It is also diurnal, which means it is active during the day. Occasionally, it can be observed in small family groups. These groups include a male, female, and two or three young. Chicks stay with their parents for about a year.

The peafowl is famous for its large tail and the colorful eye-spots on its feathers. These features are best seen when the bird fans its tail. This is quite common during the courtship display. The Congo peacock, however, does not possess this spectacular tail. But it does have a colorful display. The skin on the Congo peafowl's bare neck turns bright red during courtship then the stiff white crown of feathers on its head opens like a fan.

# PREDATORS

Predators are animals that hunt and kill other animals for food. The tropical forest has many predators living in its depths. Among them, the leopard is the largest. This predator, however, can be found in several habitats. It also lives in the savannah woodlands and areas where nonwoody vegetation mixes with grove forests. In the tropical forests, however, predators include other members of the cat family, mustelids, and viverrids. Viverrids are small, carnivorous mammals with long bodies such as civets, genets, mongooses, and others. Mustelids include such animals as weasels, skunks, otters, and badgers. Predators from the dog and hyena families are not found in the tropical forest. These animals have body structures better equipped for life in open areas. For instance, they cannot climb trees with their long paws. Instead, dogs and hyenas live in packs in the open spaces. Members of the groups depend on one another for defense and hunting. Such group behavior would be almost impossible in the dense forest.

## The Leopard

The leopard's splendid golden yellow coat with black spots is a perfect camouflage for life in the forest. Forest leopards have more brown coloring than those living in open dry areas. In fact, the famous black panther of the Asian tropical forests is merely a darker variety of the leopard. Panthers that have completely black coats are rare. For offspring to be black, both parents must be black. The gene that determines the black coloration is recessive. A recessive gene is one that is masked by other genes. So adult leopards seldom pass that trait on to offspring. In spite of this, black panthers are common in some locations. In these cases, scientists believe that the black color is a factor in helping the animal catch its prey.

Of all the members of the cat family, the leopard inhabits the largest area. It ranges from Africa to southern Asia and northward to China. Scientists have classified as many as twenty-four species of leopards.

The leopard is a successful survivor because it adapts to practically any moderately warm or tropical environment. It is found in the plains up to the snowy regions. It is found in the desert areas of North Africa and south to the humid savannahs of Uganda. The Ugandan leopard, which is one of the most magnificent species, lives there. It is found in the typical savannah woodlands and Zaire's dense tropical rain forests.

*Opposite:* The leopard is perhaps the best-known and largest forest predator. It is found in all areas of the moderately warm and tropical strips of Africa and Asia. This cat does not depend on any particular environment for its survival. In fact, in Africa the leopard is found in the rain forest as often as it is found in the open expanses of eastern savannah.

In the forest, the leopard usually ambushes its prey. In this drawing, the leopard silently stalks a bongo. The cat comes to within a few yards of its prey before leaping out and knocking the victim off balance. The leopard then finishes the kill by breaking the bongo's neck.

Leopards differ in size depending on their habitats. Those living in the savannah are larger than those living in deserts or forests. Compared to the lion, the leopard is more graceful and slender. It has a majestic appearance and is one of the most beautiful African animals. Large males measure about 8 feet (2.4 m) from the nose to the tip of the tail. They weigh about 187 pounds (85 kg). Females are smaller and lighter.

On the savannah, the leopard hunts on the ground. After a kill, the cat takes its prey in its powerful jaws and carries it up into the savannah trees. The prey may weigh as much as 155 pounds (70 kg). In the trees, the leopard can eat leisurely. There it is safe from attack by lions or packs of hyenas. On the ground, these animals will drive a leopard away from its fresh kill.

Very few studies have been made on the leopard's behavior in its tropical forest habitat. For one thing, the environment is very difficult to travel. Also, the leopard is a solitary, elusive, and silent animal. But it is known that the leopard defends a territory. Its territory may be as much as 6 sq. miles (15 sq. km) in size. The size depends on food availability in the region. In areas where food is particularly plentiful, territories may overlap. The leopard marks territorial borders by spraying its scent on low shrubs and the bases of trees. It also makes deep scratches in tree trunks. When intruders enter its territory, the leopard makes low, rasping growls as a warning.

The leopard feeds on many types of prey. Its diet includes forest antelope, bongos, bushbucks, and sitatungas that live in the swamps. It also hunts warthogs, forest pigs, pangolins, bush babies, snakes, turtles, fish, large insects, squirrels, and other rodents. It will even eat fruit if it is juicy and sweet. The leopard is sometimes known to hunt other predators. These predators are usually smaller than the leopard. They include the African golden cats, genets, and civets.

In the equatorial forest, the leopard is the main predator of monkeys and apes. It hunts those that live on the ground including baboons, chimpanzees, and gorillas. Often the leopard attacks the young of these species, but it chases adults, too. Even tree monkeys are not safe from this cat. With its powerful claws, the forest leopard climbs effortlessly up the bare lower tree trunks. Once it reaches the branches, it leaps from tree to tree. Because it is so agile, the cat moves easily among the branches. The forest leopard's

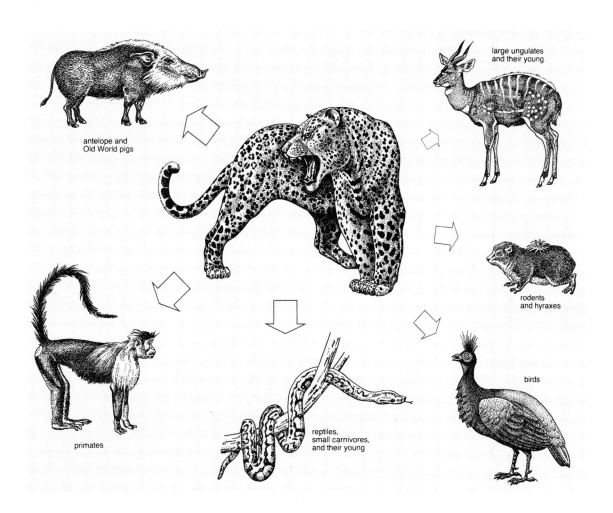

antelope and
Old World pigs

large ungulates
and their young

rodents
and hyraxes

primates

reptiles,
small carnivores,
and their young

birds

The leopard is at the top of the forest food chain. It has a diverse diet. In the drawing, the larger arrows point to prey that are most important to the leopard. It shows that its favorite prey are antelope, warthogs, and monkeys. The leopard is also a hunter of small carnivores.

size is especially helpful for hunting in this environment. This leopard is smaller than the leopard on the savannah. This allows it to catch prey which escapes to smaller tree branches. This feat would be difficult for the larger leopard of the savannah.

Because of its beautiful and valuable fur, the leopard has always been hunted relentlessly. In ancient times, this cat was found throughout the African continent. Now it is almost extinct in all of North Africa, except in large parks or very remote areas. The world population of leopards has dramatically decreased in number.

In 1973, importers and exporters of hides signed an agreement to protect certain species. The agreement is called the Convention on International Trade in Endangered Species of Wild Flora and Fauna (CITES). Under the agreement, buyers and sellers need permits to ship furs of certain endangered species. The leopard is one of these species. These rules help countries keep track of the number of animals that are being killed. If the number rises too high, a country can refuse to issue a permit. Such laws are an important step toward preserving many animal species.

## Civets and Genets

Civets and genets are carnivores. They are found throughout Africa. These small, graceful animals usually have tawny, spotted fur and large almond-shaped eyes. Their eyes are perfectly adapted to night vision. Both civets and genets belong to a family known as "viverrids." This family includes many species that live in both dry and rain forest environments.

The diet of viverrids consists mostly of insects. They also eat other invertebrates like mollusks and segmented worms. At times, they eat reptiles, amphibians, birds, and mammals. In Africa, the zibet, or large Indian civet, is common in the forests south of the Sahara Desert. It is also found in the savannah and in areas populated by people. This species is well known for the secretion with which it marks its territory. This substance gives off a very strong odor. Manufacturers of perfumes and soaps use this substance in their products. It is called "civet oil," and it produces a powerful musky odor.

Another viverrid is the giant genet. This rare species is found in the humid tropical forests of the Central African Republic, the Congo, and Uganda. Scientists first learned of it as recently as 1901. The giant genet measures about 4 feet (1.1 m) from its nose to the tip of its tail. It is the largest genet. Its yellowish coat is covered with dark spots. Its dark, bushy tail has yellow rings.

The African palm civet is the most common of all viverrid species in Africa. It is a small omnivorous predator. This civet is about the size of a cat and has a large bushy tail. It ranges over the rain forests from Guinea-Bissau on the Atlantic coast to Kenya and Mozambique. This civet is a graceful, agile climber. It moves easily over branches as its searches for insects, rodents, birds, lizards, fruit, and shoots. The palm civet has been observed climbing very smooth tree trunks and rocks. By studying its feet, scientists learned part of the reason for the palm civet's extraordinary climbing ability. It has long feet with short claws. The soles are bare and wrinkled, unlike other animals who have fur on

*Opposite:* The African palm civet is a medium-sized member of the Viverrid family. It measures 16 to 24 inches (45 to 60 cm) long. It is a tree-dweller, partly because its feet are especially suited to climbing. When it is alarmed, it jumps to the ground using a kind of flying position. Its limbs are spread out, and its tail is extended.

The drawing on this page shows two African forest cats: the western subspecies of the African golden cat *(top)* and the African wildcat *(bottom).* Some scientists believe the African wildcat is a subspecies of the European wildcat.

*Opposite:* All four of these cats are members of the Viverrid family, the small carnivores of the forest. *Clockwise from the top,* they are: The giant genet, Johnston's genet, large Indian civet or zibet, and the rare aquatic genet or Congo water civet.

the soles of their feet. These features give the palm civet an advantage when climbing.

## Small Cats

Two other cats inhabit the humid tropical forest. They are the African golden cat and the African wildcat. Both are smaller than the leopard.

Golden cats are believed to be some of the most ancient felines. The term *feline* refers to members of the cat family. Today, only three species of golden cats still exist. They are found in equatorial forests in regions quite distant from each other. They live in Africa, southern Asia, and Borneo.

The average-sized African golden cat measures 27 to 37 inches (70 to 95 cm) long. There are two subspecies of this cat. They are recognized by the color of their coats. One

has a dense brownish red coat. It inhabits an eastern region from Cameroon to Kenya. The other has gray, spotted fur. It occupies a western region from Gambia to Togo. African golden cats live alone and seldom show themselves. Little is known about their habits. However, they have been observed hunting for small prey both on the ground and in trees. They catch birds and small mammals such as dwarf antelope and dik-diks.

The African wildcat is more widely distributed than the golden cat. It is present throughout Africa, except in desert areas and Madagascar. It can live in almost any habitat where some shrubby vegetation and trees grow. In behavior and feeding patterns, this cat is very similar to the European wildcat. In fact, they are so similar that many zoologists identify them as the same species.

# WINGED INHABITANTS OF THE TROPICS

From high up in the canopy to its floor, the equatorial forest offers homes to countless numbers of animals. Of all these animals, birds have a particular advantage in finding homes. In flight, they can easily find niches at every level of the forest. A great number of bird species thrives in this favorable environment. They live on the ground. They live in the canopy. They live anywhere along the 130 to 165 feet (40 to 50 m) of foliage between those two levels.

Most animals show special adaptations to this dense, wooded environment. Even typical land vertebrates such as mammals and reptiles show adaptations. Compared to their relatives in the savannah or other regions, forest animals weigh less. Their bodies and limbs are longer so they can move easily among tree branches.

Mambas have long, slender bodies. They are an excellent example of a reptile that adapted to the forest environment. Adaptation among the mammals is seen in monkeys, squirrels, and bats. Monkeys, in particular, have long limbs and prehensile tails. A prehensile tail is one that is adapted for grabbing and holding. With its tail, the monkey can grasp tree branches, fruit, and other objects. Some squirrels' bodies have adapted in another way. Along each side of the squirrel's body, between the front and hind legs, is a membrane. This thin piece of skin is called a "patagium." When the squirrel spreads out its arms and legs in a jump, the patagium opens like butterfly wings. This makes jumping and landing easier.

## The Large Bats

A great number of bats also live in the forest. Some are much larger than average. In fact, the tropical forest Old World fruit bats are the largest in the world. Old World fruit bats are successful forest survivors of Africa and Asia. They belong to the suborder Megachiroptera. Some species are also called "flying foxes" because their muzzles resemble a fox. These are fairly large bats. They weigh over 2 pounds (1 kg) and have a wingspan of almost 5 feet (1.4 m). These bats are not found in South America.

Old World fruit bats often live in large colonies. Their daily activity begins at sunset and lasts all night. True to their name, they are fruit-eaters. They have no difficulty finding food in the tropical forest where fruit grows continually. The front side teeth, or canines, of these bats are particularly long. With them, the bats can grab fruit easily. The front teeth, called "incisors," are short and strong for

*Opposite:* A bluebilled malimbe perches near its nest. In general, the forest is an excellent habitat for all animals that can fly. By flying, birds and bats find habitats at all levels of the forest. These species do not have to fight for an ecological niche, or survival area. They find countless shelters among clusters of forest branches.

straw-colored fruit bat

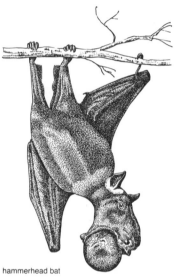

hammerhead bat

African long-tongued fruit bat

slicing through fruit skins. Bats often use their claws to bring the fruit to their mouths. They chew it with their back teeth or molars. Although they chew for a long time, bats do not eat much of the solid part of fruit. They spit out the hard fibrous parts and seeds. They eat the juice and pulp. The shape of the bat's mouth helps it eat fruit. The mouth opening is small so pulp and fruit juice do not dribble out at the corners. Tiny rasps, or scrapers, on the tongue help remove the pulp from the fruit.

The Pteroidae family of bats, called fruit bats, are some of the most common bats in the African forest. Usually, they live alone. But occasionally they are found in small groups

The flying fox pictured here belongs to a suborder known as Old World fruit bats. These large bats have a wingspan be as large as 55 inches (140 cm). Though they are found in the tropics of Africa and Asia, they are completely absent in the American tropics. They are commonly called fruit bats. But one group, the African long-tongued fruit bat, mainly eats pollen and nectar.

hanging from low tree branches during the day. At dusk, they fly off to feed. Sometimes these small groups come together and fly from one ripening fruit crop to another.

Some feed on insects. These bats have a built-in sonar system that directs them to their prey at night. Fruit bats do not have this special ability since they do not chase any prey as they fly. Instead, they are famous for being noisy.

As they eat, these bats help pollinate many forest plants. Besides fruit, these bats eat nectar, a sweet liquid found in many plants. As with other forest animals, the structure of the pollinating bat's body is like a tool for survival. It has a narrow, long muzzle and a thin elastic tongue that can go deep inside the flower. When it wants to feed, a bat lands on a flower and rests its hind legs on the lower petals. It grips the upper part of the flower with its claws. As the flower bends under the bat's weight, the nectar flows out, making feeding easy for the bat. Pollen from the flower's stamens falls on the bat's head. It is then carried to other flowers when the bat flies off.

Pollinating animals are important in the forest. Obviously, trees and plants do not move around to find mates as animals do. In order to produce seeds and new plants, they need pollen from other plants. In some places, the wind carries pollen between plants. In the tropical forest, many plants are pollinated by animals, such as bats.

Plants that depend on this method of pollination are called "chiropterophilous" plants. *Chiroterophilous* means "pollinated by bats." Since their survival depends on the bat, these plants have evolved so that their brightly-colored, sweet-smelling flowers blossom at night. Bats are attracted to these flowers by their scent and sweet nectar. In addition, these plants have flowers with sturdy, outspread petals that are easy for bats to land on.

### The Bathawk

The fruit bat takes advantage of the great amount of fruit in the forest. Likewise, a bird called the "bathawk" pursues a prey that exists in great numbers, the African forest bat.

African fruit bats have few predators. They are somewhat safe during their daytime resting period. They hang far out on thin branches that are hard for other creatures to reach. Daytime birds of prey do not bother fruit bats because these bats are active at night. Dusk is the dangerous time for bats. For at dusk, they awaken and fly from their

roosts to their feeding areas. At this time, the bathawk, which preys on bats, begins to hunt.

Because of its body structure, the bathawk cannot hunt well in the dense forest. Its long wings, narrow body, and long tail, make the bathawk a swift bird. It is a bird that needs open spaces to fly at top speed. But if the bathawk must live in open areas, how can it hunt the fruit bat? This animal lives in dense forests. The answer lies in where the bathawk lives. It lives along rivers. This unique forest habitat has two important advantages. First, above waterways, the bathawk finds open spaces for flying. Second, trees which line riverbanks provide a plentiful supply of prey.

The bathawk has a short, strong bill that tapers sharply. Because of its large mouth, it resembles the Eurasian nightjar. The Eurasian nightjar also is active at dusk and feeds on flying insects. The bathawk's long toes have strong talons which are suited for grabbing prey in flight. Its plumage is dark. Feathers on its nape form a small crest.

The bathawk roosts on a tree during the day. Sunset and dawn are its only hunting times. It flies with the speed of a falcon to the bats' feeding areas. It catches bats, large insects, and sometimes small birds in its talons. It passes the prey to its mouth and eats in flight. Large groups of insect-feeding bats find food near the river, so the bathawk does not need to go deeper into the forest to hunt fruit bats.

## Sunbirds

It is not surprising that the tropical forest has more bird species than other environments. Birds move in all directions in the thick foliage to find shelter. They move up, down, and across every level. Mammals and reptiles try to imitate the movement of birds, but they cannot match the birds' ability.

High among the upper branches of the forest is the home of tiny, brightly-colored birds known as "sunbirds." They feed on nectar and small insects that live on flowers. These birds cannot dwell at lower forest levels which are shady and dark. They must find a habitat high in the trees where sunlight allows flowers to bloom. In this level of the forest, plants known as "heliophytes" are found. These are plants that need full sunlight to thrive. Most "epiphytes" (air plants) such as orchids, ferns, and bromeliads, also grow at this level.

A great blue turaco shows off its splendid plumage and the characteristic black crest on its head. This large forest bird lives in the upper part of the foliage. There it builds its platformlike nest. Groups of five to six individuals may occupy one nest. In spite of its brilliant color and large size, the turaco is hard to sight in the forest. It lives high among the treetops. But it also is very successful at avoiding intruders. At the first sign of danger, it finds a place to hide and remains absolutely still. To observe this bird, a person must first learn to identify its loud, high call and then listen for it. At dawn and dusk, the turaco is most active.

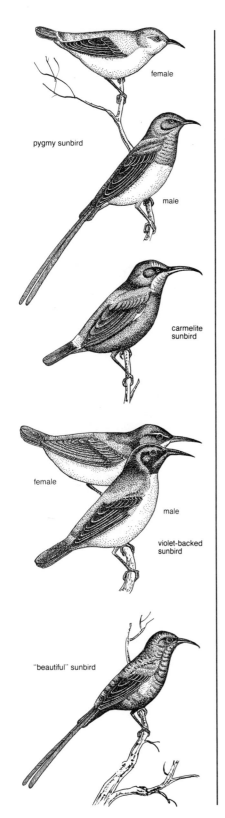

female

pygmy sunbird

male

carmelite
sunbird

female

male

violet-backed
sunbird

"beautiful" sunbird

The tiny sunbirds look like streaks of iridescent green, fiery red, and violet when speeding from flower to flower. Sunbirds live in Africa as well as in Asia and Indochina. Their counterpart in the New World is the splendid South American hummingbird.

Sunbirds eat by hovering in the air in front of a flower and plunging their long, curved bills into it. Unless they are in this position, sunbirds can scarcely be seen by humans. They are practically invisible in their natural forest habitat so high in the foliage. It is possible to spot sunbirds by standing at a clearing at the edge of the forest. Through binoculars, they are visible in flowering areas in the upper trees.

No other genus of birds has as many species as the *Nectarinia*, or long-tailed sunbirds. One very colorful species, known as the superb sunbird, is found from Sierra Leone to central Africa. Though it is only about 6 inches (14 cm) long, it is one of the largest sunbirds. Nature adorned this beautiful bird with a fiery red belly and a blue and violet throat. Its back is shaded in tones of metallic green. Its bill is long and curved. Another variety, the beautiful sunbird, is smaller. It is an extremely graceful bird with a long green tail. Numerous other long-tailed sunbirds are equally beautiful. Among them are the violet-backed sunbird and the pygmy sunbird, which has a long tail and a bright yellow belly.

## Colorful Camouflage

In a way, the tropical forest can be compared to a coral reef. Sunbirds are like the reef's most colorful fish. But both the forest's birds and the reef's fish have bright colors for special reasons. Birds recognize members of their own species partly through coloration. They also use their coloring to communicate. For example, the male bird's feathers are often brighter during the mating season. This change in coloration helps attract females. This bright coloration also serves as a warning. When a bird looking for a habitat wanders into another's territory, it quickly spots the resident bird's bright colors. This warns the intruder that the area is already occupied. Defense of a territory is very important among the birds. A family of birds depends on the food in its own territory for survival. By using colorful signals, sunbirds protect their territories without fighting. The bird's song is also used as a warning signal.

With such bright colors, it seems that sunbirds should

be easy targets for predators. Some experts say that the bright colors of the sunbirds, turacos, and tropical forest bush shrikes actually camouflage the birds from predators. But can a bird's coloring serve as camouflage, warn intruders, and attract mates all at the same time?

The answer is found by observing the location of color on these birds. Different colors appear in different places on the bird's body. For example, the bird's back is usually bright green. This camouflages it from above where birds of prey fly. Showy reds, yellows, or violets are on the breast, throat, or wingtips where smaller birds can see them. Insects near the birds may be attracted to these colors. They may mistake birds for flowers and become food for birds. Of course, the colors of tropical forest birds have many different patterns. The way these colors are arranged is a clue to the bird's habitat. A person who has studied birds can tell from its colors which niche the bird occupies.

The numerous birds that live in the canopy are among

The gaudy colors of the narina trogon stand out against the green leaves. Like most forest birds, the narina has brilliant plumage for a special reason. Because of the color, birds of the same species can immediately spot one another in a particular habitat. The color also warns birds that a particular territory is occupied. Notice that the bird's back and head are green. Its color camouflages it in the forest and keeps it safe from predators. When the bird wants to signal its presence, it lifts itself and shows the bright, contrasting colors underneath.

The African gray parrot does not have the gaudy plumage of its American relatives, macaws and blunt-tailed parrots. But it is the best "talker." Some members of this species can imitate human speech. They can sing short phrases from songs, laugh, cry, and even call people by name.

the most beautiful birds of the African continent. For example, the trogons are a family of birds that lives in the dense tropical forest habitat. The narina trogon lives in Africa. Its relative, the quetzal, lives in the mountain forests of Central and South America. In both species, the brilliant green plumage of the head and back contrasts sharply with a scarlet breast and stomach. Though they inhabit forests that are thousands of miles apart, there is only one difference between these two species. The quetzal has longer, downier wing and tail feathers than the trogan.

Deep in the forest, trogons are extremely difficult to sight. Their color blends into the foliage, but they also do not draw attention to themselves. They perch motionless on a branch. They move only to lunge at an insect or to fly to a different tree for fruit.

Turacos are lively, brilliantly-colored birds that are widespread in Africa. Many subspecies of turacas exist. The green turaco is also called the "kuyana turaco." This bird is particularly interesting because its bright colors also camouflage it. This turaco's plumage is completely green except for a large red band on its wings. It also has a thin white stripe at the edge of the tall crest on its head.

## African Parrots

About fifteen species of parrots live in Africa. The African gray parrot is a forest bird that is prized because it can imitate human speech, mechanical sounds, and the calls of other birds. This ability is so entertaining that the parrot has been hunted in great numbers and sold at high prices. As a result, it is now rarely seen in areas traveled by people.

The African gray parrot is medium-sized with white-flecked gray plumage and a bright scarlet red tail. It is more commonly found in rain forests and mangroves. But flocks can be seen flying back to their evening roosts in open fields. They eat nuts, seeds, and fruit. One of their favorite foods is oil palm fruit.

Other African parrots that belong to the genus *Poicephalus* closely resemble gray parrots. They live in the forest and are mostly green, gray, orange, or red. The rare, beautiful brown-necked parrot and Jardine's parrot are also medium-sized. They both belong to this genus. Some African parrots that live in the savannah belong to the *Poicephalus* genus. The famous parrots of the *Agapornis* genus also dwell in the savannah.

Indian white-backed vultures look for signs of food from their perches high on a tree at the forest's edge. Large raptors, such as vultures, cannot live in the dense forest. They cannot maneuver easily among the thick cluster of branches. Also, they cannot see through the thick treetops to find dead animals on the ground. Typical forest raptors are smaller, such as the goshawks, kites, and long-crested eagles. Vultures hunt in less-dense secondary forests or near clearings.

## Birds of Prey

In 1982, several scientists traveled to an area of Nigeria where fire had burned a huge section of forest. Cultivated land and wooded areas remained around the burned areas. But the burned area was bare except for a few dead trees that remained upright. The scientists decided that it was an excellent location for taking a census of birds of prey. These birds, also known as raptors, often were seen perched in the trees. From there, they could observe the surrounding area, rest, or eat their prey undisturbed. Within a few days, scientists observed more than nineteen different species of typical rain forest raptors.

Not all of these species were year-round inhabitants of

black goshawk

long-crested eagle

palm-nut vulture

red-thighed sparrow hawk

the humid tropical forest. For example, scientists spotted the black kite, the kestrel, and the honey buzzard. These are migratory birds that spend much of the year in Europe. They also saw birds that make their homes in the savannah. Although these birds do not live in the equatorial forest, they stopped in the large clearing by chance. The scientists sighted such savannah birds as Wahlberg's eagle, the tawny eagle, and the brown harrier eagle. While they were in the clearing, an osprey carrying a large fish landed on the fork of a tree and began to eat quietly. The osprey had probably caught the fish in the Niger River which is about a mile from the research area. Other species they observed such as the crowned eagle, the black goshawk, and the red-thighed sparrow hawk, were forest-bound. In other words, they survive by eating prey that lives in the heart of the forest.

The palm-nut vulture is particularly interesting. Unlike other birds of prey, it has a vegetarian diet. In appearance, the palm-nut vulture is black and white with short, rounded wings. Its wings are typical of forest birds like the northern goshawk and sparrow hawk. It is a graceful flyer. Still, gathering palm-nut fruit is not as easy as picking a ripe apple from a tree. This vulture must first find an oil or raffia palm tree. It then pulls off the hard fruit, avoiding clusters of large spines that grow near it. It breaks the fruit open with its strong beak. The palm-nut vulture also eats seafood such as mollusks and crabs. It will eat insects found in the tree foliage near its favorite fruit. This bird and the oil palm tree occupy the same territory in Africa.

# ARMY ANTS

Looking closely, visitors to the rain forest sometimes spot huge swarms of ants. Often these ants are seen moving over the ground in the shade of large trees. They are almost invisible in the dim light of the equatorial forest. The only noise they make is a faint rustling as their countless legs cross over dry leaves and twigs. At first, these dark ants look alike as they march along. But a pattern appears as they swarm. Some tightly-knit groups of ants move ahead to patrol a wide area at the head of the line. It becomes apparent that these are the well-known army ants.

Though their numbers are great, humans have nothing to fear from the army ants. Compared to people, these ants move very slowly. For their size, however, they move rather quickly. Army ants can cover about 65 feet (20 m) per hour as they fan out to explore the surrounding area in search of large insects and edible plant materials.

Army ants are widespread in all of the tropical forests. But each area has certain genuses that are found in greater numbers. In Africa, where army ants are called "driver ants," the genuses *Anomma, Dorylus,* and *Aenictus* have the most species. In South American forests, army ants are called "legionary ants." There, the genuses *Eciton, Labidus,* and *Neivamyrmex* are more common. Army ants of the *Leptogenys* genus are most common in Asia. In Australia, army ants usually belong to the *Onychomyrmex* genus.

More than 280 species of army ants have been identified to this day. Over time, these ants have developed some fascinating behaviors. Because of their special ability to organize in groups, these ants have survived in tropical forests all over the earth.

## Life in an Army Ant Colony

Perhaps the best example of ant behavior is found in African colonies of large driver ants of the species *Anomma wilwerthi.* A colony consists of a queen, soldiers, workers, and young ants. It may contain anywhere from ten thousand to several million members. Compared to the worker ants, the queens are giants. They can measure up to 2 inches (50 mm) long.

Driver ants tend to be nomadic. They do not nest in one area but move periodically to new hunting sites. When not on the move, they build complicated underground nests that can be from 3 to 13 feet (1 to 4 m) deep. There they stay for about twenty days while the queen ant lays her eggs. She lays hundreds or even thousands of eggs at one time. Then

*Opposite:* Army ants march together in a dense column across an opening in a Zambian forest. Millions of these ants make up a single colony. They all work together in a highly-organized way. For this reason, they are particularly fascinating to study. Ant columns become a kind of superorganism which can totally wipe out the food resources of large areas.

99

The drawing shows, in correct proportion, the body structures of the various ants of the *Anomma* genus. Social insects, such as ants, have various types of members within the same species. The members are divided into castes, or social positions, according to their function in the society. Their physical characteristics vary according to their roles. Even among the workers, there are differences. Some of these differences are related to what groups within the colony eat. Larger workers attack larger prey. Smaller workers feed on small insects and larvae. In this way, a colony can usually take advantage of different types of prey that are driven out by raids. The drawing on the opposite page shows patterns of advance and retreat of raiding swarms from a temporary shelter.

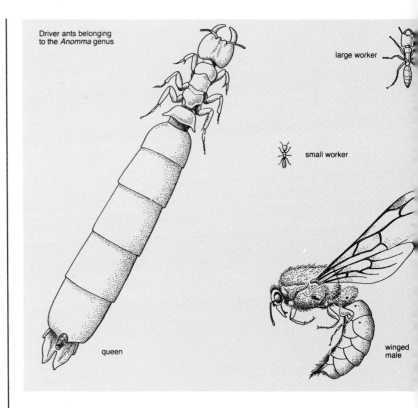

Driver ants belonging to the *Anomma* genus

large worker

small worker

queen

winged male

the entire colony, consisting of millions of ants, moves on. For about two or three days, these ants travel day and night for a distance of 650 to 1,000 feet (200 to 300 m).

While traveling, the huge group of worker ants work together, carrying the queen and her brood. The brood consists mostly of pupae, which are ants that are not fully grown. Then the colony stops to build a new underground nest for the queen and waits for another twenty or twenty-five days. During their stops, swarms made up of millions of ants leave the nest. They raid the surrounding territory for prey.

As with other army ants, ants of the *Anomma* species raid in a highly-organized way. First, the swarm groups around the nest and forms an advance line, about 40 feet (12 m) wide. Next, the swarm narrows into a column and wanders for a few yards. Finally, it branches out into a fan-shaped front. The advance line drives out any prey in its path and catches it. This raiding group may contain several million ants, including the workers which rush ahead so that the line is always moving outward. As the millions of tiny legs move over the leaves, they make a characteristic

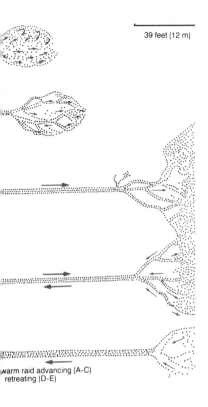

39 feet (12 m)

warm raid advancing (A-C)
retreating (D-E)

rustling and crackling sound.

At the same time, other insects are disturbed by the raid. Grasshoppers and large beetles jump and scurry to escape the ants. Many large insects such as flies and mosquitoes buzz around the advancing ants, ready to prey on insects they flush out.

Driver ants prey mostly on arthropods, a large group of invertebrates. This group includes spiders and insects such as grasshoppers, roaches, and crickets. But in some cases, they will kill and eat larger animals that cannot escape quickly. These may include small reptiles, bird nestlings, small mammals, and reptiles that are digesting prey.

Scientists have observed that army ants "clean up" wide areas of the forest as they advance. Studies of the forest floor show that after a raid by army ants, the number of insects on the forest floor is reduced. However, the effect is temporary. In a short time, the cleared area is once again taken over by populations of insects that live nearby.

After a raid by a colony of *Anomma* ants, food resources in the area near their nests are quickly reduced. The ants are forced to march on to a new territory. Other species, such as the *Eciton* of the Amazon forests, may search much

Tiny forest spiders are one of the favorite prey of army ants. After an ant column has passed over an area, there is a drastic reduction in the population of insects. With little food available, the colony is forced to move on to new hunting territory. However, nearby populations of insects rapidly take over the vacant area.

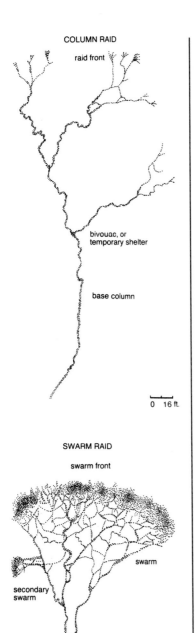

COLUMN RAID

raid front

bivouac, or
temporary shelter

base column

0    16 ft.

SWARM RAID

swarm front

swarm

secondary
swarm

base column

bivouac

0    16 ft.

longer for new hunting grounds. These ants may travel for up to seventeen days. During this time, they may nest at a new site every night.

## Cooperating to Survive

In tropical forests all over the world, a great number of ant species behave like the driver ants described above. It seems that they are at a great disadvantage because they must move to new feeding areas so often. The must carry the large queen and young which cannot move on their own. Why is this method of survival so successful? The answer is that ants work together in large groups. Because of this cooperation, they easily obtain prey that one or a few ants could never catch. Army ants can attack, kill, and devour

large prey. But ants that hunt alone can only catch prey their own size.

Groups of ants are able to kill prey that are tens and hundreds of times larger than themselves. Typically, they invade other ant nests. But sometimes they even attack wasp nests. Some army ants also eat one type of prey in particular. For example, ants of the *Megaponera* genus usually attack termite mounds.

# GUIDE TO AREAS OF NATURAL INTEREST

A visit to the African tropical forest environment is strikingly different from a trip to the open savannah. Travelers to the grasslands can easily observe giraffes galloping in the distance and lions resting lazily during the day. In the equatorial forest, however, travel is much more difficult. People must make their way through the dense vegetation to observe the animals and plants. But there are some locations where forest animals and plants can be seen more easily. For example, travel is easier in areas where the trees or layers of plant cover have been cleared. Also, by following a path near a native village, or one that wild animals use, a person can pass through the "green wall" to experience the forest firsthand. But most often, paths do not exist.

Probably the fastest way for a visitor to observe the forest environment is by water. Small rivers and their tributaries often cross the forest and lead into dense areas that are not accessible by other means.

Within the tropical forest, many animals are almost invisible because of their camouflaging coloration. Snakes such as the mamba or the gaboon viper are particularly difficult to see. Although it is important to be aware of the danger, visitors should know that people seldom encounter snakes. These reptiles generally avoid people. Insects and parasites are found everywhere. These are the real danger because they carry diseases. For example, the tsetse fly is a forest insect that transmits sleeping sickness. Before the trip, travelers should have the necessary vaccinations and follow precautions to avoid malaria. Visitors to the forest must also be careful to drink only fresh, running water. They must be careful that bathing water is not contaminated.

Some of the areas listed in this guide are in very dense forest areas. Some of the areas are so dense that there are no tourist facilities. However, many areas offer various types of comfortable lodging. Some offer well-equipped, permanent campgrounds. It should be noted that several equatorial parks and reserves of Africa have sections of clearings and savannah mixed with areas of thick forest. Where these open areas exist, the forest is easier to reach. Visitors who have the equipment may camp there safely.

*Opposite:* Natives use a dugout canoe, called a pirogue, for fishing and transportation. Here they cross the Niger River Delta. One of the world's largest mangrove forests grows in this delta. Lush plant life grows near the warm tropical waters, and an abundance of marine life lives in the water. The human population is increasing in Niger, as it is in many areas near the forest. The survival of the forest and its wildlife is threatened as more and more people use the forest to grow profitable crops, harvest trees, and build settlements.

## IVORY COAST

Mount Nimba (1)

This natural reserve was established in 1943 and is fully protected. It shares borders with Liberia and the Republic of Guinea and includes an area of about 20 sq. miles (50 sq. km) that rises 1,640 to 5,740 feet (500 to 1,750 m)

*Right:* The map shows some of equatorial Africa's most important areas of natural interest. These parks and reserves are not completely covered with virgin forest. Today, areas of savannah and sparse scrub trees replace sections of the original forest throughout tropical Africa.

*Below:* This map shows the area covered by forest vegetation in Africa.

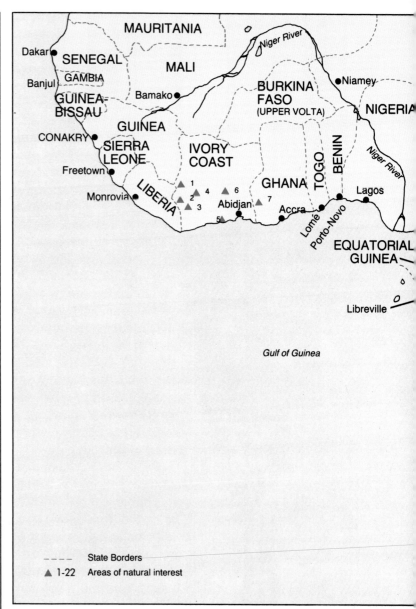

in altitude. The environment is very interesting. At low altitudes, there is a dense humid tropical forest. This becomes a gallery forest in valleys at altitudes from 3,280 to 5,250 feet (1,000 to 1,600 m) high. Grass of the *Londetia* genus is plentiful in the higher zones.

Mammals living in this reserve are pottos, Senegal bush babies, chimpanzees, otters, large Indian civets, African golden cats, leopards, and warthogs. A particularly interesting amphibian that can be found in this reserve is

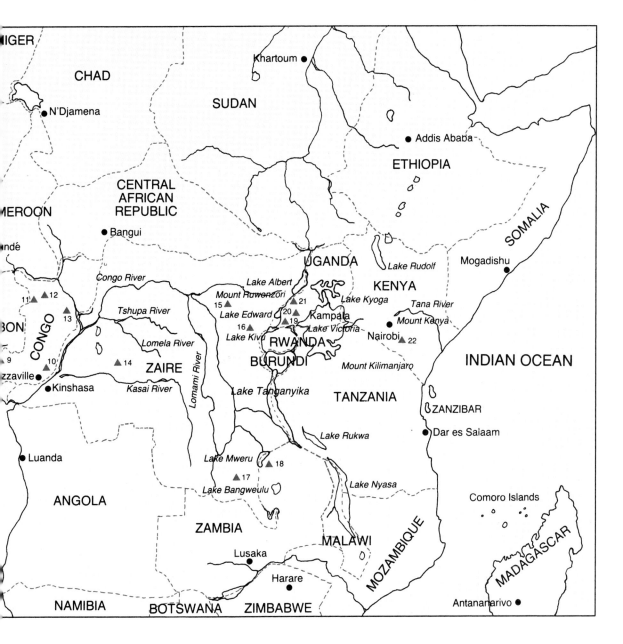

the live-bearing toad. The young of this toad are born fully developed. It lives in the mountain grasslands at altitudes between 3,940 and 5,250 feet (1,200 to 1,600 m). Many species of birds are native to the area.

The reserve does not have tourist facilities or trails.

Established in 1972, this wildlife reserve is partially protected. It is 282 sq. miles (730 sq. km) in area at an altitude between 328 and 820 feet (100 to 250 m). Its location

N'Zo (2)

is about 93 miles (150 km) south of Man. Exploitation of the forest, or use for hunting, growing, or other business reasons, is allowed in this area. The reserve and the nearby park called Taï are similar. It is mostly flat except for a few isolated hills formed by the process of intrusion. During intrusion, molten rock was forced between layers of existing rock and pushed upward, creating these hills.

A definite dry season lasts from December to February. The vegetation consists of dense evergreen forest with trees that grow about 130 to 200 feet (40 to 60 m) high. An abundance of epiphytes and lianas grow there. Tree trunks have characteristic support buttresses and strut-like aerial roots. The dominant species of trees are the ebony, the *Parinari cheyrophylla*, and the palm *Ermospathe macrocarpa*. Among the wildlife are various tree monkey species. Rare species like the pygmy hippopotamus, and various duikers including Jentink's duiker and the banded duiker live here.

The reserve does not have tourist facilities, and access is difficult. However, it can be reached from the north by Taï Park or by boat on the N'Zo River, a tributary of the Sassandra.

---

**Taï (3)**

---

Established in 1972, this reserve is located about 124 miles (200 km) south of Man, and 62 miles (100 km) from the coast. It lies between the Cavally River and Liberia. Its eastern border is the Sassandra River. This national park covers 1,274 sq. miles (3,300 sq. km). It is a sloping granite plain dotted with a few isolated hills formed during volcanic eruptions.

Dense evergreen forest vegetation is everywhere. Tall trees rise about 130 to 200 feet (40 to 60 m) high. They have massive tree trunks supported by wide buttresses or strut-like aerial roots. Epiphytes and lianas are particularly abundant on these trees. This reserve has two main types of forest. The palm forest contains the *Parinari* and *Diospyros* genuses that are typical of the poorer northern soils. The Sassandra forest in the southwest features various species of ebony and other marshland species. The park's mammals include numerous guenons, colobus monkeys, chimpanzees, various pangolins, leopards, and African golden cats. There are also pygmy hippopotamuses and giant forest pigs. An extraordinary number of duikers, bongos, and royal antelope live here.

The park is close to Man, the region's largest population center of the region. Transportation is available to the nearby rain forest. Some tourist facilities are available in the area south of the park around Mount Niénokouë.

## Mount Peko (4)

Established in 1968, this national park lies about 75 miles, (120 km) southeast of Man and covers about 130 sq. miles (340 sq. km). The mountainous region has peaks that rise higher than 3,280 feet (1,000 m). The main waterways are the tributaries of the Sassandra River. The river flows about 7 miles (12 km) east of the protected border area.

About 80 percent of the park territory is covered by dense seasonal forests. Here the most common species of trees are mahogany, limba, and the oak *Lophira lanceolata*. About 20 percent of the park consists of savannah woodland that grew after the forest was destroyed. Endangered species such as the chimpanzee, leopard, and baboon are commonly seen in this park. The giant pangolin and water chevrotain live in the region but are rarely seen.

No facilities for tourists exist in the park. Visitors stay at Man which has the closest available lodging and transportation. The park is located some distance from the highway that runs between Man and Daloa.

## Banco (5)

This fully protected national park was established in 1926. It covers about 12 sq. miles (30 sq. km). It is located on the western bank of the Ebrié Lagoon, near the mouth of the Banco River. It is about 6 miles (10 km) west of Abidjan. People who live in the city often visit Banco because sections of the park have been developed for recreation. The park is very interesting to visit. Visitors can walk on the park's 37 miles (60 km) of trails or visit the botanic garden. The natural surroundings consist of a dense rain forest and, in open areas, some mahogany plantations. Congo whitenosed guenons, chimpanzees, black-and-white colobus monkeys, large Indian civets, genets, and Maxwell's duikers live in the park. In general, wildlife is not plentiful.

## Marahoué (6)

Located in the west central region of the Ivory Coast, this 386 sq. mile (1,000 sq. km) national park was established in 1968. The park is located north of the Bouaflé-Daloa Road, along the Marahoué River. It is a region of low rolling hills that is crossed by the Marahoué River and its tributaries on the south. A large lake formed by the Bandama Blanc Dam separates the park from other territories.

In the park's eastern and northeastern sections, savan-

nah occupies one-third of the protected territory. The remaining two-thirds in the south and southeast are occupied by dense seasonal forests and some gallery forests. Flora and fauna species that are characteristic of both the forest and the savannah are in the park. Mammals in the park include baboons, guenons, colobus monkeys, and chimpanzees. There is also a modest number of African elephants, large reedbucks, and bongos.

The park can be reached from the west by a paved highway that connects with the northbound highway at Yamoussoukro. The main entrance is at Gobazra, and there are special trails for tourists. Yamoussoukro and Daloa have hotel accommodations.

# GHANA

## Bia (7)

Established in 1974, this national park covers over 117 sq. miles (302 sq. km). It lies in the eastern Ivory Coast region between the country's border and the Bia River. It is important because this may be the only area in Ghana where humid tropical forest still exists. It is the only location where many species of plants and animals that are native to Ghana can survive. In this forest a definite dry season lasts from December to March. Temperatures in the area vary from highs of 84° to 93°F (29° to 34°C) in July and August, to lows of 68° to 71°F (20° to 22°C) in February and March.

Vegetation in the park consists mainly of genuses of the *Celtis-Triplochiton* groupings usually found in semideciduous humid rain forests. Flower species such as *Raphia vinifera, Raphia gigantea,* and many other epiphytic orchids grow in this park. Mammals present in the park include three species of colobus monkeys, Diana monkeys, chimpanzees, leopards, African elephants, giant duikers, bongos, bushbucks, dwarf buffalos, and giant forest pigs. Many of these species would be completely extinct in Ghana if this forest were destroyed or altered.

Visitors come to this park even though it is not well known. Tourist facilities are being built within the park.

# GABON

## Wonga-Wonguaa (8)

Established in 1967, this national park covers an area of about 1,400 sq. miles (3,600 sq. km). It is located on the Atlantic Coast between Libreville and Port-Gentil, west of Lambaréné. The park's altitude is between 3,280 and 5,250 feet (1,000 and 1,600 m) above sea level. It includes crystalline rock hills of the Sierra del Cristal coastal area. There marshland stretches between the rocky ridges. Vegetation is typical of a humid tropical forest. Ebony and other hardwood species such as *Copaifera mopana* and palms of the genus *Calamus* grow here. Vast areas of scrubby savannah woodland are present on plateaus. The forest contains gaboon mahogany, *ilomba*, limba, and iroko.

The chimpanzee is common in this park. There are also lowland gorillas, African elephants, aquatic chevrotains, and sitatungas. Visitors may also see reptiles such as the python and the gaboon viper.

# CONGO

## North and South Nyanga (9)

These two wildlife reserves were established in 1958. Together they cover 158 sq. miles (410 sq. km). They are located in Divénié, a district in south-central Congo south of the Nyanga River. Savannah covers most of the land surface. But about a quarter of the area is occupied by gallery forests and limba forests. Few tourists have visited the area to see splendid Lake Tsoubon, known for its deep waters, or the narrow and scenic Mitsoubon Gorge.

The region's climate is equatorial and humid. It averages about 98 to 117 inches (2,500 to 3,000 mm) of rainfall annually. The fauna has not been studied much but includes the bush pig, hippopotamus, sitatunga, African buffalo, bushbuck, and the defassa waterbuck.

## Lefini (10)

This region has been a wildlife reserve since 1951. It covers about 3,667 sq. miles (9,500 sq. km) between the Bateke plateaus and the Pool region. It is located about 78 miles (125 km) north of Brazzaville. Its vast sandstone plains are carved by rivers that flow throughout the year in gorges that are 650 to 1,000 feet (200 to 300 m) deep. Dense tropical forests cover these canyons, making the area very scenic. At times the forest meets plateaus covered with open, treeless grasslands. This savannah is crossed by the Lefini and Nambouli rivers, two of the Congo River's largest tributaries. The fauna consists mainly of savannah species. But in forest areas there are guenons, duikers, forest elephants, and dwarf buffalos. This reserve has no tourist facilities except for a small rest area.

## Odzala (11)

Established in 1940, this national park covers 424 sq. miles (1,100 sq. km) in northwest Congo. It is located about 19 miles (30 km) from the Gabon border and 75 miles (120 km) southwest of Ouesso, on the Cameroon border. The

A group of tourists climbs a trail inside the Ruwenzori Forest, Uganda. The environment shown is typical of the secondary forest. New trees have grown since the original forest was cleared. In the virgin forest, visitors must follow established trails or let a guide cut a path. The thick vegetation makes it difficult to observe plants and wildlife even when standing in the forest. Visitors hear sounds of wildlife more often than they actually see anything.

terrain of the park is hilly in the south and rather flat in the north. Secondary tropical forest grows in most areas except on hilly ridges where savannah has taken over. Interesting species of wildlife make their habitats in Odzala. There are chimpanzees and gorillas as well as leopards and African golden cats. Ungulates such as giant forest pigs, bush pigs, bongos, various duikers, and dwarf buffalos can also be seen here.

## Lekoli-Pandaka (12)

This wildlife reserve in the northwest Congo covers about 193 sq. miles (500 sq. km). It is at an altitude of 650 to 985 feet (200 to 300 m). The reserve is located about 93 miles (150 km) southwest of Ouesso at the Cameroon border. Equatorial rain forest covers about 70 percent of the reserve. The remaining area is savannah where tall grass, low bushes, and scattered trees grow.

During the rainy season, which lasts for nine months, the ground is soaked with water. During that time, landslides and erosion are common and more than half of the reserve is flooded. Average temperatures vary between 73° and 82°F (23° and 28°C). Mammals include various primates, lions, leopards, African elephants, giant forest pigs, bongos, bushbucks, bush pigs, and various duikers.

The reserve is not yet open to the public.

## M'bomo (13)

This reserve is located in the Congo's Cuvette region. It was established in 1955 on an area of 347 sq. miles (900 sq. km). It is near the Lekoli-Pandaka Reserve where the Ubangi and Congo rivers meet. Savannah covers 80 percent of the reserve. Humid tropical forests remain in small sections. Thunderstorms occur frequently during the rainy season. Because wood was considered very valuable, many trees have been cut down and sold for wood. Now few trees remain. Wildlife in this forest consists mainly of colobus monkeys, guenons, forest elephants, bushbucks, and dwarf buffalos.

Few tourists visit the reserve. No special facilities for them exist. Controlled hunting is allowed.

# ZAIRE

## Salonga (14)

This large national park covers about 14,000 sq. miles (36,260 sq. km). It is completely protected. Established in 1970, it is located in Zaire's central Congo River Basin. It has an altitude of 1,150 to 2,500 feet (350 to 760 m). Preserved here are three different types of landscape: low plateaus, terraces produced by rivers, and high plateaus. The average daily temperature ranges from 68°F (20°C) at night to about 90°F (32°C) during the day. An uninhabited area between the Loile and Luilaka rivers about 25 miles (40 km) wide divides the national park in two.

Three types of equatorial forest grow in this large region: swampy, rainy, and semideciduous forest. In the northern sector, grasses are the most common vegetation. The last of the rare and endangered dwarf chimpanzees make their home in this area of Zaire. Other mammals include rare species of guenons, leopards, and forest elephants. Birds include the African wood ibis, the Congo peafowl, and the openbill. Among the reptiles that find refuge in Salonga is the African slender-snouted crocodile. This animal also is close to extinction.

The park is accessible to tourists only by river.

## Maiko (15)

Still inaccessible to tourists, this intact nature reserve was established in 1970. It covers about 3,860 sq. miles (10,000 sq. km) of land. It is located in a semimountainous region of eastern Zaire that reaches altitudes between 2,300 and 4,265 feet (700 to 1,300 m). The reserve lies between the central Congo River Basin and the western mountains of the Great Rift Valley. This area is the most humid in Zaire because no dry seasons occur and rainfall is abundant. The south and north sections of the reserve are hilly. The center is flat. The park's vegetation consists of dense, humid equatorial forests. These are a transition phase between the forests of the plains in the Congo River Basin and mountain forests. Among the plentiful wildlife are three rare forest species: the mountain gorilla, the okapi, and the Congo peafowl. African elephants, cape buffalos, and duikers also live here.

## Kahuzi-Biega (16)

This national park is located west of Bukavu in eastern Zaire. It occupies about 232 sq. miles (600 sq. km) and is 3,280 to 9,840 feet (1,000 to 3,000 m) high. The park is fully protected. It includes western mountains of the Great Rift Valley that lie within the Congo River Basin between Walungu and Massisi. In the west, a hilly transition area extends from the plains forests to mountain forests. Mountain forests cover most of the park. Virgin forests cover two-thirds of the area. Some bamboo and low underbrush, especially on higher ground, is mixed in with the forest vegetation. The rest of the territory is covered with meso-

With its elegant black-and-yellow body, the Jameson's mamba moves easily through the tree branches. Its coloring camouflages it among the forest vegetation. People seldom see these extremely-poisonous snakes when hiking through the forest. At the slightest sign of an intruder, the mamba flees. It attacks only when threatened or if it senses that an intruder is not keeping a safe distance.

phytic forests. These are forests that require a moderate amount of water. Tall trees of the *Hagenia* genus are found here. The park's main attraction is the 250 mountain gorillas that live there. One or two of the gorilla groups are used to being watched by the tourists. Visitors also can observe chimpanzees, numerous guenons, and colobus monkeys. Giant forest pigs and herds of African elephants also live here. There are as many as one hundred elephants in a single herd here.

This park was established in 1970 in southeastern Zaire. It covers an area of 850 sq. miles (2,200 sq. km) and lies between 3,940 and 5,575 feet (1,200 and 1,700 m) in altitude. Its plant life and wildlife are fully protected. The region is composed of highlands like the plateau of the Shaba region. At the park's western border, steep cliffs drop 1,310 feet (400 m) to the Lufira River Valley. Scenic waterfalls, said to be the highest in Africa, are fed by the Logoi, a tributary of the Lufira River. They fall from 1,122 feet (342 m).

The vegetation is mostly savannah. Thin forests and gallery forests along rivers grow here. At least fifteen species of ungulates live in this park. They include zebras and numerous antelope. The reserve also includes various guenons and baboons, felines such as the leopard and cheetah, and birds such as hornbills and wattled cranes.

The park is open to the public. Travelers can enter by way of Lubumbashi and proceed by cross-country vehicle on the roads. At Katwe, there is a landing strip for light planes. Campsites are available in the surrounding area.

## Kundelungu (17)

# ZAMBIA

## Lusenga (18)

This national park was established in 1972. It occupies 340 sq. miles (880 sq. km) north of Kawambwa in the province of Luapula. It is between 2,625 and 4,265 feet (800 and 1,300 m) in altitude. Part of the park is covered by savannahs and part by swampy, evergreen forests. These forests are characterized by trees of the *Marquesia* genus which can survive during dry seasons. However, dense forests also grow in Lusenga. The wildlife in Lusenga is not plentiful. But populations of grass monkeys and Diana monkeys, leopards, zebras, warthogs, bushbucks, elands, forest duikers, reedbucks, and buffalos still make the park their habitat.

It is difficult to travel in the park because the roads are poor. But there are two camping grounds just outside the park's borders near the waterfalls of the Kalungwishi River.

# UGANDA

## Gorilla (19)

## Kigezi (20)

## Kibale (21)

Gorilla is one of the smaller reserves. It occupies about 19 sq. miles (48 sq. km). It was established in 1964 for the protection of the mountain gorilla and chimpanzee. It is located in the extreme southwestern corner of Uganda, between 8,860 and 13,448 feet (2,700 and 4,100 m) in altitude. Within its territory are three forest-covered volcanic mountains: the Muhavura, the Mgahinga, and the Sabinio. The highest point of the reserve is at the peak of Muhavura with its beautiful crater lake. Shrubby vegetation such as heather and Klamath weed is found on the high peaks. Below the peaks, thinner mountain forests alternate with shrubby growth and bamboo thickets. Savannah woodland grows on lower slopes. Many interesting animals live here. Among the wildlife are chimpanzees and mountain gorillas, a rare subspecies of blue monkey, leopards, giant forest pigs, and bushbucks. There are many bird species here, including the Ruwenzori turaco, six species of sunbirds, and five species of waxbills.

The reserve is about 50 miles (80 km) from Kabale which has comfortable hotel facilities.

Established in 1952, this reserve occupies 127 sq. miles (330 sq. km) at an altitude of about 3,280 feet (1,000 m). Its southern portion is adjacent to Ruwenzori Park. Most of Kigezi is covered by a vast plain where only a few trees grow. But part of this reserve includes the southern section of the Maremagambo Forest. In that location, the main vegetation is seasonal forest and savannah grassland. Acacia and albizzias trees are common. Mammals include lions, leopards, African elephants, warthogs, giant forest pigs, hippopotamuses, and an eastern subspecies of the chimpanzee.

Visitors can enter the park by taking the road out of Kabale that leads into Ruwenzori Park. Typical African savannah can be seen on the way. Permanent settlements are not allowed inside the park. Hunting is authorized only by special permits.

This area was set aside as a reserve in 1964. It covers an area of 12 sq. miles (32 sq. km) at an altitude between 2,952 and 3,280 feet (900 and 1,000 m). It is located north of Ruwenzori Park and Lake George as far as Fort Portal. The reserve is covered by humid, semideciduous forest that thins out and becomes savannah with sparse trees and bushes. Beyond the savannah is an open plain. Animals of

the Ruwenzori National Park migrate in and out of Kibale. This makes the few animal populations unstable. Among the species found are elephants, giant forest pigs, hippopotamuses, dwarf buffalos, waterbucks, leopards, and many tree monkeys.

Limited hunting is allowed, but tourists are not permitted to enter.

# KENYA

---

Doinyo Sabuk (22)

---

This national park was established in 1967. It is located northeast of Nairobi. The park includes an area of 7 sq. miles (18 sq. km) at an altitude between 4,920 and 7,055 feet (1,500 and 2,150 m). Rising from the nearby plains is a single granite mountain known as an "inselberg." It was formed during the Paleozoic era. Mountain forest covers the mountain. Plants of the genus *Olea*, the Podocarpus genus, and crotons are commonly found here. Mammals include black-and-white colobus monkeys, leopards, black rhinoceroses, bushbucks, and impalas. Among the many birds species in this park is the spectacular great blue turaco.

Located near the city of Nairobi, the park is a popular tourist attraction. Visitors usually come for day trips. But those who wish to stay in the park may use one of two camping areas.

*Preceding pages:* The mountain forest is perhaps the most amazing and fascinating area of the African equatorial forest. Mountain forests extend below the snow line at altitudes between 11,480 and 14,100 feet (3,500 and 4,300 m). There the temperature averages about 53° to 59°F (12° to 15°C). Rainfall is scarce because these forests are above the usual cloud cover. However, the air surrounding these lofty tropical forests is very humid. Fog often blankets the forest.

# GLOSSARY

**abundant** very plentiful; more than enough.

**aggressive** inclined to start fights or quarrels.

**algae** primitive organisms which resemble plants but do not have true roots, stems, or leaves.

**anthropoid** resembling humans; humanlike.

**atmosphere** the gaseous mass surrounding the earth. The atmosphere consists of oxygen, nitrogen, and other gases, and extends to a height of about 22,000 miles (35,000 kilometers).

**australopithecene** of or relating to a genus of extinct apelike people from southern Africa who made tools and walked in an upright position.

**basin** all the land drained by a river and its branches.

**biosphere** the zone of the earth extending from its crust out into the surrounding atmosphere which contains living organisms.

**botanist** a person who specializes in plant life.

**camouflage** a disguise or concealment of any kind.

**canopy** anything that covers or seems to cover, like an awning or other rooflike structure.

**conservation** the controlled use and systematic protection of natural resources, such as forests and waterways.

**continent** one of the principal land masses of the earth. Africa, Antarctica, Asia, Europe, North America, South America, and Australia are regarded as continents.

**deciduous forests** forests having trees that shed their leaves at a specific season or stage of growth.

**deforestation** the clearing of forests or trees.

**diurnal** active during the day.

**dominant** that species of plant or animal which is most numerous in a community, and which has control over the other organisms in its environment.

**dormant** alive, but not actively growing; in a state of suspended animation.

**ecology** the relationship between organisms and their environment.

**environment** the circumstances or conditions of a plant or animal's surroundings. The physical and social conditions of an organism's environment influences its growth and development.

**epiphyte** a plant, such as certain orchids or ferns, that grows on another plant upon which it depends for physical support but not for nutrients.

**equator** an imaginary circle around the earth, equally distant at all points from both the North Pole and the South Pole.

**ethologist** a scientist or specialist who studies the characteristic behavior patterns of animals.

**extinction** the process of destroying or extinguishing.

**famine** an acute shortage of food.

**fauna** the animals of a particular region or period.

**genus** a classification of plants or animals with common distinguishing characteristics. A genus is the main subdivision of a family and is made up of a small group of closely related species or of a single species.

**gregarious** living in herds, flocks, or some other group.

**habitat** the areas or type of environment in which a person or other organism normally occurs.

**herbivore** an animal that eats plants.

**humid** containing a large amount of water or water vapor.

**hydrophyte** any plant growing only in water or very wet earth.

**invertebrate** lacking a backbone or spinal column.

**liana** any thick, woody, tropical vine that roots in the ground and climbs around tree trunks.

**lichen** primitive plants formed by the association of blue-green algae with fungi.

**mustelids** fur-bearing mammals.

**nectar** the sweet liquid in many flowers, used by bees for the making of honey.

**niche** the specific space occupied by an organism within its habitat; a small space or hollow.

**nocturnal** referring to animals that are active at night.

**nomads** people who do not have a permanent home.

**omnivore** an animal that eats both plants and other animals.

**ornithologist** a specialist or scientist who studies birds.

**parasite** an organism that grows, feeds, and is sheltered on or in a different organism, while contributing nothing to the survival of its host.

**precipitation** water droplets or ice particles condensed from water vapor in the atmosphere, producing rain or snow that falls to the earth's surface.

**predator** an animal that lives by preying on others. Predators kill other animals for food.

**prehensile** adapted for seizing or grasping, especially by wrapping or folding around something.

**primate** any of an order of mammals, including humans, apes, and monkeys.

**Pygmy** a person belonging to any of several modern African and Asian peoples of small stature.

**rain forest** a dense, evergreen forest occupying a tropical region having abundant rainfall throughout the year.

**rodent** any of an order of animals, characterized by constantly growing teeth adapted for chewing or nibbling.

**ruminants** cud-chewing animals; grazing animals having a stomach with four chambers.

**savanna** a treeless plain or a grassland characterized by scattered trees, especially in tropical or subtropical regions having seasonal rains.

**species** a distinct kind, sort, variety, or class.

**stomata** openings on a leaf which allow it to expel excess moisture and continue the process of respiration.

**talon** the claw of a bird of prey or other predatory animal.

**tropophytic** able to adjust to conditions of heat or cold, dryness or moisture, etc., as in seasonal changes. Rain forests are also called "tropophytic forests."

**ungulate** of or belonging to a group of animals which have hooves.

**vertebrate** having a backbone or spinal column. Fish, amphibians, reptiles, birds, and mammals are primarily vertebrates, having a segmented body or a spinal column.

**xerophyte** a plant structurally adapted to growing under very dry or desert conditions, often having smaller leaf surfaces for avoiding water loss, thick fleshy parts for water storage, and hairs, spines, or thorns.

**zoologist** a specialist in the study of animals; their life structure, growth, and classification.

# INDEX

## CREDITS

**MAPS AND DRAWINGS.** G. Vaccaro, Cologna Veneta (VR). **PHOTOGRAPHS. A. Borroni,** Milan: M. Mairani 112-113. **Diamonde,** Turin: P. Visintini 8, 18-19. Marka Graphic, Milan: 12-13,50. **Overseas,** Milan: Jacana/J.P.Champroux 20, 40-41, 43, 64-65, 102-103; Jacana/Devez 46-47, 81, 84, 90-91,94-95, 116-117; Jacana/Hervy 71; Jacana/J. Jacana 58-59; Jacana/ R. Jacana 66-67, Jacana/J.P. Varin 88; Jacana; J.P. Varin A. Visage 35, 48-49, 68; Jacana/A. Visage 34; Jacana/Ziesler 93; Oxford Scientific Films/D. Curl 86-87. **Panda Photo,** Rome: C. Consiglio 32; G. Tognon 10; A. Zocchi 120-121; WWF International/P. Oberle 52. **L. Pellegrini,** Milan: 6-7, 15, 17, 22-23, 28-29, 62, 72-73, 96-97, 98, 104. **L. Ricciarini,** Milan: J.L. Grande sovraccoperta. **F. Speranza,** Milan: 57; A. Calegari 42, 101; Pioli-Pirovano 27, 54, 110. **M.P. Stradella,** Milan: studio Pizzi 24-25, 39. **F. Veronesi,** Segrate (MI): 76.